Slaveries of the
First Millennium

PAST IMPERFECT

See further
www.arc-humanities.org/our-series/pi

Slaveries of the First Millennium

Youval Rotman

British Library Cataloguing in Publication Data
A catalogue record for this book is available from the British Library

ISBN (print) 9781641891714
e-ISBN (PDF) 9781641891721
e-ISBN (EPUB) 9781641891738

www.arc-humanities.org
Printed and bound in the UK (by CPI Group [UK] Ltd), USA (by Bookmasters), and elsewhere using print-on-demand technology.

Contents

Introduction

Whence Slavery?

If we try to imagine what slavery looks like, we will probably visualize black cotton pickers, chained Africans coerced into slave ships, Roman gladiators, slave markets in modern Libya, girls and women forced into a life of prostitution, children undertaking hard manual labour. For many of us the term slavery resonates a horrific experience of harsh exploitation in a way that restricts personal freedom and dignity. If we look for images on the internet, we will probably get the same results. Such images reflect the modern concept of slavery, which is composed of stories, histories, education, political awareness, and is also fed by the news. All of these conditions are based on acts of enslavement that reduce a human being to a tool, a device, a piece of merchandise, a means of profit and exploitation, in ways that contradict human rights, freedom, and dignity, a severe crime against a human being.

The perception of slavery as a crime against humanity is a product of the nineteenth-century abolitionist movement that fought with great success to eradicate slavery from the world. Its objective was to end phenomena that existed throughout history in myriad societies, phenomena that although very different one from another, had in common the legalization of the enslavement of human beings. The fight for the eradication of slavery went hand in hand with the development of the human rights movement. Yet, what appeared in the twentieth century as a great international political success seems in the twenty-first century now just wishful thinking. The current human rights discourse refers to "modern slavery" or "contemporary slavery" and publicizes modern forms of enslavement that have become frequent over the last thirty years. This raises a disturbing question: is slavery back? And if so, are we dealing with the same kind of phenomenon, the same slavery?

To take a recent case, in January 2019 a federal jury convicted the couple Mohamed Toure and Denise Cros-Toure of Southlake, Texas, for the forced labour of a Guinean girl for sixteen years. Three months later they were sentenced to seven years in prison each and $288,620.24 in restitution. The couple brought the girl from her Guinean village in 2000 and forced her to work without pay in their home as a housekeeper, cook, and nanny. The case was tried as a case of *forced labour*, meaning work which a person is coerced to provide against their will.

Another famous case is "The Queen v Wei Tang" in 2006, in which the Australian Court of Justice convicted the owner of a licensed brothel in Melbourne of five counts of intentionally possessing a slave and five counts of intentionally exercising a power of ownership over a slave. Tang was the first person convicted under anti-slavery laws that had been introduced in 1999.[1] She was accused of having purchased five women from Thailand to work in *debt bondage* in her brothel, and was sentenced to ten years in prison. The women had agreements with a broker in Thailand. He passed them on to Tang by selling her these "contracts" for twenty thousand Australian dollars. The women arrived in Australia separately in 2002 to 2003 on tourist visas, each owing forty to forty-five thousand Australian dollars to the owner of these "contracts." Their debt was reduced by fifty dollars per customer. They worked six days a week for long hours. They were not locked up, but their passports were retained. Since their visas had been obtained illegally, they feared detection by immigration authorities. The debt bondage that Tang applied to the women formed the basis of the charges of slavery.

---

1 Details of both cases are provided at the end of the Further Reading section at the end.

Both cases were individual, private acts of enslavement that were tried as illegal. Other cases show that bondage and enslavement can become normalized. A particularly extreme form of bondage is practised today in the global fishing industry. Southeast Asian fisheries can trap migrant workers illegally and hold them as *enslaved labourers* for years, sometimes for life. Cut off from their home and having lost their status as citizens, on a foreign fishing vessel on the open seas where there is no way of escape, no legal authority, and *de facto* no legal status, these workers experience years of severe living conditions, sexual assault, harsh violence, even murder. Working under dubious agreements or wilfully ignored by the relevant state for reasons of profit, this form of enslavement differs from the two previous cases. It represents a significant part of the economies of Southeast Asian countries and the global economy.[2]

Another form of enslavement that is also inherent to socioeconomic structures and falls within legal norms is the bonded labour of children trapped in the brick industry in Pakistan and India.[3] Kiln managers and owners provide loans to workers who are unable to repay them, and so they become *bonded labourers* of their debt owners. They can

---

2 V. A. Prum, *The Dead Eye and the Deep Blue Sea: A Graphic Memoir of Modern Slavery* (New York: Seven Stories, 2018). Also *Blood and Water: Human Rights Abuse in the Global Seafood Industry* (London: Environmental Justice Foundation, 2019): https://ejfoundation.org/resources/downloads/Blood-water-06-2019-final.pdf (accessed June 5, 2020).

3 Bales, *Disposable People*, 149–94. A. Ercelawn and M. Nauman, "Unfree Labour in South Asia: Debt Bondage at Brick Kilns in Pakistan," *Economic and Political Weekly* 39, no. 22 (2004): 2235–42. S. Kumari, "Neo-Bondage in the Brick Kiln Industry: A Case Study of Bihar," *Social Change* 48, no. 3 (2018): 384–97. A. Bhukuth, "Child Labour and Debt Bondage: A Case Study of Brick Kiln Workers in Southeast India," *Journal of Asian and African Studies* 40, no. 4 (2005): 287–302. Also see https://www.aljazeera.com/indepth/features/spiraling-debt-trapping-pakistan-brick-kiln-workers–190903135224452.html (accessed February 1, 2020).

be transferred from one creditor to another and become trapped in perpetual debt bondage that they unwillingly pass onto their children.

We may ask in what way these contemporary examples are different from the images we have of chattel slavery through which enslaved humans become merchandise, and are bought, sold, and dominated exclusively by their enslavers. Indeed, slavery is often defined as any type of exertion of ownership, possession, or trading of human beings, their body, life, and labour. Enslaved persons are considered victims whose life has been changed forever by their subjugation to an enslaver.[4]

Slavery has been declared illegal in most countries (as we shall see in the next chapter). The International Convention on Slavery of 1926 refers to slavery as "the status or condition of a person over whom any or all of the powers attaching to the right of ownership are exercised."[5] Although slavery is illegal today, different forms of enslavement, such as bondage, forced labour, and human trafficking (trade in humans for the purpose of their enslavement) are very much part of today's world, and are normalized or legalized (such as the bondage mentioned above in fisheries and the kilns). Can we define them all as slavery? This question troubles scholars, historians, sociologists, anthropologists, advocates, human-rights activists, and politicians. Are we speaking of new forms of slavery in today's world? And if so, how do they relate to historical forms of slavery?

In view of such questions it is not surprising that the study of slavery has undergone a paradigm shift over the last two decades. This has arisen as recent scholarship in history, the social sciences, law, and human rights has responded to the questions that modern phenomena of enslavement, bondage, and human trafficking evoke, such as: What is the difference between ownership and possession, between slavery

---

4 O. Patterson, *Slavery and Social Death: A Comparative Study* (Cambridge, MA: Harvard University Press, 1982).

5 League of Nations Slavery Convention, §1.1.

de jure and *de facto*, between slavery and enslavement? How do we define human trafficking, and what is voluntary and involuntary enslavement? From historical and anthropological perspectives too scholars emphasize the different definitions that slavery can have and the different conditions it creates. In consequence, since the end of the twentieth century we have obtained a far more diverse and richer picture about slavery and the different forms of enslavement that it supports.[6]

In this respect we may distinguish between enslavement and slavery in the following manner: enslavement is the act and the state of reducing persons, their labour, and the product of their labour, to a thing which the enslaver can possess, own, use, exploit, exchange, emancipate, or transfer to another. Slavery, on the other hand, is the system that creates, enables, normalizes, and maintains such situations and relationships. In other words, enslavement is the actual state of the enslaved person, while slavery is the framework, the system, that supports it.

Social history has focused on the understanding of such systems throughout the long history of humanity, has revealed the conditions and rationales that create phenomena of enslavement, and has explained how and why their normalization and institutionalization occur in particular societies. Scholarship paints a complex picture of the different purposes, changing conditions, and the versatile role of slavery in different historical circumstances, and challenges us to consider this diversity, its dynamics, and versatility to be in themselves the essence of slavery, its particular character.

How can we analyze the versatile, adaptive character of slavery as a system? The societies of the first millennium around the Mediterranean, Europe, and the Middle East, offer an ideal case-study. The first millennium was a period of tremendous transformation in every respect: geopolitical, social, economic, legal, cultural, religious, intellectual. In so

6 Miller, *The Problem of Slavery as History*. Shelley, *Human Trafficking*. Condominas, ed. *Formes extrêmes de dépendance*.

many ways these transformations determined how the map would look like for centuries to come, and their outcomes are still with us today. Slavery played a central role in these processes of transformation. But, according to the common historical periodization ancient forms of slavery, Greek and Roman in particular, get studied together, while slaveries after the sixth century are cut off from their Antique and Late Antique antecedents.

The present study adopts a new perspective in choosing an uncommon historical framework in which the slavery of the Roman Empire is analyzed together with slaveries in the developing medieval societies that followed it. A broad historical perspective that bridges two periods is essential in order to examine in what ways slavery became instrumental to historical development. Slavery had been used as a way to construct the new Empire. It was later used to structure and form new medieval societies, economies, and cultures. Adopting a long historical perspective will enable us to study these different forms of slavery together and to examine the way in which the adaptable character of slavery was used in the broad process of transformation of Antiquity into the Middle Ages.

It is not easy to accept the idea that slavery played such a pivotal and active role in our past, mainly because we consider it today as a crime against humanity. However, understanding the role that slavery played in historical transformations will help us to perceive slavery not only as a social phenomenon, but as a historical process. This can shed new light also on questions relating to our modern world and the place that slavery occupies in it. Because contemporary forms of enslavement are rarely institutionalized but are often the result of clandestine or individual private activities, we might get the impression that enslavement is back but not slavery. Yet, the cases of bondage in fisheries or of brick workers, cited above, show us that enslavement today is normalized and plays an integral part in the socioeconomic dynamics of certain societies. In order to eradicate them, we need to understand the specific functions they fulfill and that make them profitable. What conditions and circumstances make slavery more profitable and productive than other types of labour or exploitation? Although modern slavery does not constitute a large part in the global economy today, it is certainly on the rise. Our historical perspective will reveal slavery to be a historical process.

The five chapters of this book follow chronologically the history of the Mediterranean during the first millennium, focusing on different forms of slavery that developed in the civilizations that composed it and were connected to it. The Mediterranean of the first millennium presents a unique historical case for such a study. It was the venue for significant historical transformations thanks to its dense populations, rich economies, and its political complexities. Slavery played a major role in all this.

Chapter 1, "From Present to Past and Back," is a theoretical introduction adopting a retrospective analysis. It examines different perspectives in the study of slavery and presents a new approach that challenges the monolithic definition of slavery. It presents diverse types of slavery and indicates those conditions that make it important to historical evolution.

Chapter 2, "Slavery between Two Phenomena: Empire and Christianity," examines the way slavery influenced the development of the two major historical phenomena of the first centuries of the first millennium: the consolidation of the Roman Empire and the crystallization of Christianity until the two merged in the form of a new Christian Romano-Byzantine Empire. It deals with the changes that slavery brought to the perception of the individual and it challenges the concept of a "slave owning society," a rhetorical concept that historians have artificially used to link ancient slavery to modern American slavery.

Chapter 3, "Enslavement, Captivity, and the Monotheistic Turn," examines the role of enslavement in the transformation of the Roman Empire into a world of distinct medieval monotheistic civilizations: Byzantium, the Caliphates, the Germanic kingdoms of Latin Western Europe. It challenges the idea of a decline of slavery and examines how slavery changed between Antiquity and the Middle Ages.

Chapter 4, "New Polities, New Societies, New Economies," looks at the social and economic foundations of the new medieval societies. It traces the central roles that slaveries played in each of them in the period of their formation and reveals the adaptable character of slavery as a means of economic development.

Chapter 5, "Migration, Integration, Connectivity," traces a global, international framework during the Central Middle Ages as a way of explaining how the different forms of slavery related to each other. It reveals slavery not only as a means to establish new social structures in new societies and new economies, but also for their connectivity. Studying how slavery relates to voluntary migration, forced migration, and connectivity between people and economies reveals its global aspect.

* * *

If we want to fight for the eradication of modern slavery we first need to understand its significance as a form of exploitation, adaptable to changing circumstances. The purpose of this book is to challenge perspectives that look at slavery as a discrete phenomenon and instead to examine the historical development of the first millennium through the eyes of slavery. Perceiving slavery not just as a social phenomenon but as a system that enabled the development of historical societies and emerging economies will reveal the role it plays as a historical process.

Chapter I

From Present to Past and Back

Slavery has existed throughout history in different parts of the world and across different societies. Its exact definition is a matter of debate, as is the question of whether the entire range of historical and modern phenomena known as slavery can be narrowed down to a single definition. What is accepted, however, is the fact that throughout history societies have systematized the ownership and possession of human beings, their lives, and their labour within legal, social, economic, and cultural frameworks, and profited from their exploitation and trade.[1] Although slavery does not exist legally in any of the member states of the United Nations today, reference to "contemporary forms of slavery" has become widespread over the last two decades. Different phenomena of human exploitation, bondage, trafficking, and commodifying, as well as *de facto* possessing of human beings are now termed "modern slavery." This leads to a theoretical problem in studying the conditions that constitute slavery: what is the difference between defining it *de jure* and *de facto*? This question has troubled scholars of slavery, jurists, judges, and lawyers (Kotiswaran, *Revisiting the Law*).

Slavery was defined in the 1926 Convention of the League of Nations, which by 2013 had been ratified by ninety-nine states. Its first article defines slavery as follows: "(1) Slavery is the status or condition of a person over whom any or all of the powers

---

1 Michael Zeuske, *Sklaverei: Eine Menschheitsgeschichte von der Steinzeit bis heute* (Ditzingen: Reclam, 2018).

attaching to the right of ownership are exercised. (2) The slave trade includes all acts involved in the capture, acquisition or disposal of a person with intent to reduce him to slavery; all acts involved in the acquisition of a slave with a view to selling or exchanging him; all acts of disposal by sale or exchange of a slave acquired with a view to being sold or exchanged, and, in general, every act of trade or transport in slaves."

Slavery is defined *de jure* in most legal codes in modern states and is punishable. Facing a growing number of phenomena that are perceived as modern slavery, contemporary legal systems require criteria that will enable judges to decide whether a particular form of human exploitation, trafficking, possession, or merchandising has occurred and whether it falls under the legal definition of slavery and is therefore a crime. In other words, the main question is how to identify what I will term here as *"de facto* slavery." For example, although ownership of human beings is illegal, a court of law nevertheless has to decide when a person exerts ownership on another person in a way that contravenes the law. This is no different from any other criminal offence. However, unlike any other criminal offence, the international political premise is that *de facto* slavery exists nearly everywhere in today's world, and that the legal system both nationally and internationally is responsible for its eradication. In the eyes of the law and international political discourse this makes modern slavery resemble organized crime.

Modern slavery shares another feature with organized crime: its rationale is economic. Slavery is profitable. The enslaved are exploited for the economic value of their activities, their human bodies, or their movement. According to the 2017 Annual Report of the International Labour Organization (ILO), 24.9 million people are today victims of forced labour, while 15.4 million people are victims of forced marriage. 71 percent of the former are girls and women; 25 percent are children. Half of these are exploited by private individuals or enterprises in a state of debt bondage. Of those exploited by individuals or enterprises, 4.8 million are victims of forced sexual exploitation. These figures, accurate or not, reveal a worldwide network that sustains and profits from modern slavery: there is a global economic rationale to the enslavement of millions of people today.

Modern slavery is also a matter of modern scholarship. In 1999, sociologist and economist Kevin Bales published his landmark *Disposable People: New Slavery in the Global Economy*. Bales offers a first-hand account of the operations of five slave-based businesses: prostitution of girls in Thailand sold by their parents to pimps, selling of water by enslaved persons in Mauritania, workers in the production of charcoal in Brazil, bonded farmers in India who traded their freedom of movement for a parcel of land to cultivate, and families held in perpetual bondage in brickmaking in Pakistan due to the debt they inherited. The book had an astounding impact on world opinion towards contemporary forms of slavery. It was nominated for the Pulitzer Prize and was published in ten languages. In contrast to other accounts of modern forms of slavery, which centre on human rights violations, Bales adopted a socioeconomic perspective and exposed them as products of specific social structures and legal conditions.

Disposable People provoked the issue of *de facto* slavery in contrast to *de jure* slavery. All the examples refer to people who were not illegally enslaved, victims of illegal kidnapping, human trafficking, nor were forced to work against the law. The forms of their exploitation were legal. They were the products of the way in which the legal systems in their countries functioned, and could not be defined legally as slaves. However, for Bales, they did form *de facto* slavery. The intention of Bales, co-founder and past president of "Free the Slaves," an international non-governmental organization (NGO) and lobby group, was to raise awareness of modern practices of slavery around the world. For him the need to identify forms of exploitation as slavery is connected to changes that micro-social systems have undergone in the world of globalized economies. Defining slavery is a means to perceive, conceptualize, and address problems spawned by a global economy.[2]

---

2 See the Bellagio–Harvard Guidelines on the Legal Parameters of Slavery.

And yet, insisting on the global economic rationale behind modern slavery and putting it in the same frame as organized crime may lead us to ignore a vital aspect of the phenomenon and its dynamics: the fact that it can exist as a built-in phenomenon in a given society. Indeed, *de facto* slavery is detectable on the micro level more than the macro level. One of the main questions that calls for examination is how the two are connected. Bales argues that the systems employed in a globalized economy create local conditions that sustain local forms of slavery. However, slavery has existed in different forms on a micro level regardless of a globalized context, as anthropological studies on slavery reveal.

In 1998, a year prior to Bales' publication, Georges Condominas, a French anthropologist, published a collection of anthropological and historical studies under the (Anglicized) title: *Extreme Forms of Dependency: A Contribution to the Study of Slavery in Southeast Asia*. It marked a new line of thought in the anthropology of slavery. These studies, as well as those that followed in their footsteps, aimed at examining societies in which the terms slaves and slavery were not readily apparent and did not fall under a legal definition of slavery, yet they still involved extreme forms of exploitation, which played a particular role in the dynamics of their social framework. Taking a broad view of social dependency, such research foregrounded the social, economic, and juridical conditions that generate extreme forms of dependency, and ask if and how these forms can be termed slavery. From deciphering Khmer inscriptions of the Angkor kingdom through investigating secluded tribes in the Philippines to considering the descendants of slaves in Madagascar, these studies reveal the need to move beyond accepted (*de jure*) macro definitions of slavery to micro-societies. They demonstrate how, in the course of their development, distinct societies produce the economic and legal conditions for human subjugation. Like political activists and advocates, anthropologists too are required to identify phenomena of slavery. The question is by what criteria.

Changing Perspectives:
Slavery as a Social Institution

Taking as an example "the National Referral Mechanism" (NRM) in the United Kingdom, we can acknowledge what criteria are used today to define *de facto* slavery. The NRM is a framework whose role is to identify victims of human trafficking, slavery, servitude, and forced or compulsory labour, and to ensure that they receive the appropriate legal protection and support. It was introduced in 2009 to meet the UK's obligations under the Council of Europe's Convention on Action against Trafficking in Human Beings. According to the NRM's definitions for a person to have been a victim of human trafficking three requirements must apply. First, an action: recruitment, transportation, transfer, harbouring, or receipt, which can include either domestic or cross-border movement. Second, a means: an individual is held, either physically or through threat of penalty, by a means, such as threat or use of force, coercion, abduction, fraud, deception, abuse of power, or vulnerability. Third, a purpose of exploitation: namely that a service is provided for benefit, such as sexual exploitation, forced labour, or domestic servitude, slavery, removal of organs, begging, sexual services, manual labour, domestic service (see UK Home Office's statutory guidance on modern slavery, 2016).

The UK's NRM is not unique. Most official organizations and NGOs founded with the objective of combatting modern slavery follow the same approach. They use criteria that pertain to illegal forms of dependency which severely restrict human rights. The terms servitude, enslavement, bondage, debt slavery, forced labour, coerced labour, coercion, chattel slavery, human trafficking, human merchandising, sexual trafficking, and forced marriage are used in order to refer to different aspects of a global notion of what constitutes slavery. These aspects are used as criteria to identify slavery, and as a way to fight it. Indeed, the human rights and political discourses about slavery and scholarship on the subject all share a common political and moral agenda: slavery is a crime against humanity that needs to be fought against until its eradication. This approach, shared by political activists, legislators, economists, historians, anthropologists, political scientists, and sociologists, is an outcome of a moral perception of slavery and a political agenda inherited from the abolitionist movement.[3]

We should all share such an attitude and perspective: possession, ownership, trafficking, merchandising, and commodifying human beings are crimes against humanity, and we must find the means, theoretical as practical, to fight them. And yet, defining slavery according to a political agenda that aims at its eradication and applying moral criteria to identify it, could lead us to a narrow perspective when we come to analyze different forms of slavery. We see slavery as a negative intrusion, a phenomenon that, like organized crime, is perceived as an external un-organic intervention into normal social conduct, rather than as an integral part of a social system. This may lead us to ignore important parts of the picture: the multifaceted functions of slavery, the different roles that it is assigned to play in different societies, its functions, and purposes. Although we define it today as a crime, in the long history of slavery this perception is an exception. History and anthropology can help enlarge our social and moral perception of slavery.

In *Slavery in Africa: Historical and Anthropological Perspectives* Suzanna Miers and Igor Kopytoff introduced the notion of slavery as a means of social integration of foreigners in a way that was complementary to kinship, arguing for a "slavery-to-kinship continuum." Slavery, in this perspective, is not a socioeconomic class defined by a legal status as Marx would have it. A decade later, Claude Meillasoux (*The Anthropology of Slavery*) contrasted slavery with kinship as a means of gaining economic and political power. Slavery, for him, constitutes a class of people with no control over their reproduction. These two seemingly conflictual theories show the

---

3 General Assembly of the United Nations, "The Protocol to Prevent, Suppress and Punish Trafficking […]." U.S. Department of State 2018 Trafficking in Persons Report.

spectrum through which slavery is perceived and studied. Although slavery is today a crime, its socioeconomic rationale and the ways it was used in processes of social development must be analyzed if we seek its eradication. In other words, we need to understand the role that slavery plays in order to replace it with alternatives avoiding enslavement of fellow human beings. We must understand what makes enslavement purposeful in order to fight it successfully. To do that we need to study societies that institutionalized it. In other words, we need to understand the logic of systems of slavery so as to develop strategies and means to fight the enslavers on their terrain of human exploitation, control, and coercion.

Today, political, human rights, and advocacy discourses use legal and socioeconomic criteria to identify servitude, forced labour, enslavement, bondage, debt slavery, human trafficking, and human merchandising. All these concepts refer to socioeconomic relations of inequality by which one person subjugates another in a way that restricts their status and allows their exploitation. Thus, exploitation in its socioeconomic meaning depends on inequality of status. Here lies the main difficulty in defining slavery: not every form of exploitation based on inequality is slavery and slavery, despite its economic rationale, does not necessarily depend on exploitation. How then should we define exploitation and what is the difference between exploitation and slavery? As we have seen above, to identify cases of exploitation as *de facto* slavery the NRM looks for purposes, means, actions, and services. Unfortunately, this approach, shared by advocates, NGOs, and activists, reveals the main problem with methods to identify *de facto* slavery: they do not explain how forms of exploitation defined as slavery turn into a system and become a "social institution."

Contemporary sociologists use the term social institution to refer to a complex social form that can reproduce itself.[4]

---

[4] S. Miller, "Social Institutions," *The Stanford Encyclopedia of Philosophy*: https://plato.stanford.edu/archives/sum2019/entries/social-institutions/ (accessed August 30, 2019).

We can define social institutions as phenomena which play a fundamental role in a social structure, system, and organization, and influence the behaviour of individuals within a given society. The dynamics of a social system depend on its institutions. Take for example marriage, government, schools, prisons, the postal service, the law, ownership, prostitution, the mafia, kingship; they all share a similar function: they define social behaviour and determine aspects of social dynamics. They are therefore factors in the social environment. The question is what makes forms of enslavement institutionalized, or in other words: how can we trace slavery as a social institution? This does not necessarily require that slavery be legal. Human trafficking, for example, albeit illegal determines the social dynamics and personal conditions of millions of people around the world today.[5] It becomes an institution once it becomes a factor in the social structure and determines social behaviour. Moreover, it also affects the social, economic, cultural, and legal dynamics of societies which, as it were, benefit from human trafficking. In a similar way, the commodifying of people by restricting their human rights plays a role in today's international labour market and affects the economic structure of societies which profit from it. Though mostly illegal, such forms of modern slavery play a role in socioeconomic dynamics: social development becomes dependent on the institutionalization of forms of enslavement.

History helps to reveal this hidden side of socioeconomic development which slavery facilitates.

Using the Plural Form:
From Slavery to Slaveries

The human rights and political discourse about slavery that has developed over the last two decades has radically changed our concept of what constituted slavery. The vast literature and scholarship on slavery show a wide array of definitions that conclude that slavery is a dynamic social phe-

---

5 Shelley, *Human Trafficking*. Bravo, "Exploring the Analogy."

nomenon which can appear in distinct social environments and serve different socioeconomic functions. This perspective has influenced the way historians approach, identify, and analyze slavery. If fifty years ago scholars were seeking a single definition to cover Roman slavery, antebellum American slavery, and slavery in the Caribbean colonies, to take familiar examples, today this approach is no longer tenable. Historians have become more aware of the diversity behind slavery and are looking to study its different forms and its versatile character in order to identify the different roles it played in human history. In other words, today we refer not to slavery, but to slaveries.

Moreover, the long timespan of history reveals the place that slaveries and the enslaved held in the development of varied societies. Historians analyze the processes of institutionalization behind forms of enslavement. Moving from the past to the present helps us analyze the development of forms of enslavement today. For example, identifying how forced migration, labour migrants, as well as precarious conditions of refugees are connected, can lead us to acknowledge the ways in which *de facto* slavery is being systematized in the ways we deal today with the status of migrants and refugees (Shelley, *Human Trafficking*).

Our modern perception of what constitutes slavery today leaves a large grey area for numerous phenomena that benefit from enslavement and lead to its institutionalization. It is essential to study the history of such processes to understand how and why they occur. This is all the more important for societies where slavery was not a crime and used it in different ways and for different purposes as part of their social, economic, political, and cultural life. Such an analysis reveals the different rationales that sustain slavery, and sheds new light on the question why slavery has returned, and what connects *de jure* and *de facto* slavery. Taking a broad historical scope allows us to follow not only the institutionalization of enslavement, but also its determinant conditions: how and why does it change.

Slavery as Historical Process

My purpose in this book is to address the problem and definition of slavery through a study of the role it played as a historical process. I propose to challenge current perspectives about slavery by placing historical development at the heart of the discussion and by explaining it from the perspective of slavery. I aim to present the social rationale of slavery as a historical process. So, this study aims at revealing the conditions that made slavery important in history. I propose to take the history of the Mediterranean world of the first millennium CE as a framework.

The first millennium witnessed the foundation of a single civilization around the Mediterranean: the Roman Empire. Its formation required new social, economic, and cultural structures. Slavery played a central role. At the same time, the rise of Christianity led to changes of and adaptations to Roman social structures. The assimilation of Church and State and the foundation of a new Roman capital in Constantinople resulted in the formation of a new millennium-long civilization: what we call today Byzantium. This was only the first stage in the long transformation of the Roman Mediterranean into a world of distinct monotheistic civilizations, a process that I term here "the monotheistic turn."

The "barbarian invasions" of the fourth to seventh centuries, their formation into new Christian states, the development of Rabbinic Judaism, and the advent of Islam reshaped the world and transformed the Greco-Roman civilization into a medieval world divided between four monotheistic civilizations: the Greek Empire of Byzantium, the Muslim Caliphate, Latin Western Europe, and the Jewish communities. These civilizations were distinct in their social and economic structures. Mediterranean societies were the most populated and the most advanced economies of this part of the globe. They created sophisticated cultures. From Cordova to Constantinople, Rome to Cairo and Baghdad, they established vibrant intellectual life, and founded new, diverse, and complex political institutions.

In each of these civilizations slavery took on a new form. The slaveries of medieval Western Europe, Central Europe, the Balkans, the Middle East, the Iberian Peninsula, and North Africa were different from each other. Enslavement, trafficking, commodifying, owning, and possessing of human beings were omnipresent in all these societies. They played an important role in the formation of their socioeconomic structures and their specific historical development. The Mediterranean of the first millennium offers an ideal framework to analyze the phenomenon of slaveries as a historical process.

Such an objective also calls for a new historical perspective. Instead of explaining the history of slavery in view of the geopolitical changes of the first millennium, I propose to proceed the other way round and to consider the historical evolution of the first millennium from the angle of slavery, the enslaved, and the enslaver. My main question is therefore what did slavery offer to the historical evolution of the first millennium, what made it a vital phenomenon. The diversity of slavery on the one hand and the role it played in the historical evolution of the Mediterranean world in the first millennium on the other hand, will show slavery as a flexible, adaptable, and dynamic phenomenon: that is, a historical process.[6]

Questions of Methodology

Examining slavery as a historical process over a timespan of a millennium during which the Mediterranean world had radically changed its structures, means following different paths along the historical process of slavery. This study explores and analyzes distinct Mediterranean societies, economies, and cultures that shared a common ancient past as well as a common international present, and were dependent on each other. From this perspective, for example, Byzantine slavery will take its place in the global historical process of slavery in relation to the Roman institution of slavery that it inherited. Moreover, a comparative approach will allow us to ana-

---

6 Cf. Miller, *The Problem of Slavery as History*.

lyze it together with the Muslim institutions of slavery, the international medieval slave trade, as well as in relation to other Christian and pagan societies at that time. Such a perspective focuses on threads between slaveries in distinct yet connected societies. This requires a comparative methodology that is synchronic and follows the historical evolution of these different cultures from the first millennium together. In this way we can detect what changes slavery underwent and reveal the factors that have made it a historical process. On the other hand, this perspective also requires a diachronic approach (examining a phenomenon over time), especially by analyzing what internal socioeconomic factors determined the role that slavery played in the historical development of medieval cultures.

When we make diachronic comparisons, we are dealing with forms of enslavement in societies that, although distinct, share a common historical framework. Legal definitions, social and economic criteria, as well as cultural constructs will reveal the ways in which forms of enslavements were institutionalized to form a system.

* * *

The experience of slavery is a cruel one, and has marked the lives, minds, and souls of millions of children, women, and men through the history of the Mediterranean and the entire world. These people were victims of this historical process and are considered victims in our discourse today, but they were not always considered as such in their own day. We cannot refer to the historical process of slavery without referring to its victims. Indeed, the questions who the enslaved were, where they came from, in what ways their status marked their lives and their place within their societies, and for what and for whose benefit, are pertinent questions not only to understand the experience of slavery, but also to understand the dynamics of slavery as a historical process.

The next four chapters follow chronologically the evolution of the Mediterranean world throughout the first millennium. They examine the ways in which slavery formed one of the main historical processes that shaped this evolution. They reveal how slavery interacted with and determined Mediterranean history. Since historical processes are made up of and affect people's lives, this investigation will relate to girls, boys, women, men, young and old, family ties, household structures, governmental structures and institutions, rulers, economic structures, wages and labour, bondage, trafficking, as well as dependency in varying forms, and the concept of freedom in its legal, social, economic, cultural, and psychological aspects. Since our approach is chronological we begin with the historical process of slavery and its role within the two central historical phenomena of the first four centuries of the first millennium: the Roman Empire and Christianity.

Chapter 2

Slavery between Two Phenomena: Empire and Christianity

First to Fourth Centuries

In his second-century compilation of legal "institutes" the Roman jurist Gaius classified the different statuses of men as follows: "The main classification in the law of persons (Latin: *jus personarum*) is this: all men are either free (*liberi*) or slaves (*servi*). Again, among free men (*liberi homines*), some are free-born (*ingenui*) while others are freed (*libertini*). Free-born are those who were born free; freedmen, those who have been manumitted from lawful slavery. There are three kinds of freedmen: for they are either Roman citizens, or Latins or in the category of capitulated aliens (*dediticii*, i.e. who have in the past taken up arms and fought against the Roman people and then surrendered after defeat)" (*The Institutes of Gaius*, bk. 1, tit. 3–5).

This text goes on to describe in length the circumstances pertaining to each. It elaborates on the social states of the enslaved referring to slaves who were chained as a form of punishment, interrogated under torture, handed over to fight in gladiatorial combats with swords or with beasts. It refers to the legal forms by which slaves were manumitted (freed as legally freed persons). A manumitted male slave could become agent (*procurator*) of his owner and so act on his behalf. Female slaves (*anchillae*) could be manumitted for the purpose of marriage (since Roman marriage only existed between two free persons). Slaves could be also manumitted in the owner's will. They could become Roman citizens and inherit from their enslavers.[1]

Unlike the different circumstances of slaves, the different types of freedmen entailed different legal statuses. There were those who were given the status of Latins ("assimilated to the Latins of the colonies") who could not make a will for themselves, inherit, or be appointed as guardians in a will.[2] There were "capitulated aliens" (*dediticii*) who could not be granted Roman citizenship and their presence in the city of Rome was forbidden. Gaius' first Institute made clear that slavery was part of a large array of legal statuses that made up Roman society.

In comparison to this elaborated definition of legal categories and the social states and the distinct statuses that they constituted, the biblical New Testament offers a contrasting definition: "For when all of you were baptized into Christ, you put on Christ as though he were your clothing. There is neither Jew nor pagan; there is neither slave nor free; there is no male and female, for all of you are One in Christ Jesus" (Galatians 3:27–28). At first sight this verse expresses an egalitarian approach for the community of believers: once baptized no social categorization exists, a true social revolution. Yet, the meaning of this revolutionary message was less clear. Christianity was open to everyone, including slaves. Slaves could become Christians like everyone else, but it did not follow that they were to be freed and legally constituted as equals.

Paul treats this subject in his Letter to Philomen concerning Philomen's slave Onesimos (literally "the useful"), who ran away and found refuge with Paul. Despite pleading with Philomen to treat his slave as a beloved brother in Christ, Paul still sends Onesimos back to Philomen.[3] Receiving, helping,

---

1 *The Institutes of Gaius*, bk. 1, tit. 6–7. Buckland, *The Roman Law of Slavery*, 437–48.

2 Buckland, *The Roman Law of Slavery*, 553–51.

3 This has received different interpretations: J. Albert Harrill, *Slaves in the New Testament: Literary, Social, and Moral Dimensions* (Minneapolis: Fortress, 2006). De Wet, *The Unbound God*. Glancy, *Slavery in Early Christianity*.

and keeping a fugitive slave was a punishable crime. Paul concludes the apostolic Christian attitude towards slaves in his Letter to Titus 2:9–11: "slaves (Greek: *douloi*) are to be submissive to their own masters (*despotes*) in everything; they are to be well-pleasing, not argumentative, not pilfering, but showing all good faith, so that in everything they may adorn the doctrine of God our Savior. For the grace of God has appeared, bringing salvation for all people."

The same attitude appears in the Letter to the Ephesians (6:5). Paul urges the slave to "be obedient to them who are your masters according to the flesh, with fear and trembling, in singleness of your heart as unto Christ." So, the duty of the enslaved to be submissive is a duty towards God, while the enslavers should be considerate towards their slaves, which is also a duty towards God (Colossians 4:1). Thus Paul's egalitarian message in his Letter to the Galatians is a religious one: no classification of religious statuses exists within Christian society. Yet, since Roman society required slavery it was attributed a spiritual meaning in Christian discourse. It was God's will that made a person enslaved or enslaver (Garnsey, *Ideas of Slavery from Aristotle to Augustine*). And this rationale served as a justification for preserving the inequality between the enslaver and the enslaved, even when both were Christians.

A priori there is no contradiction between the Roman and Christian worlds, nor between the laws of the state and the newly established Christian doctrine. However, the two do not treat the enslavement of human beings in the same way. While the laws of the Empire are interested in legal and social categorization, Christianity constructs an alternative concept of society in which the existing social categorization reflects a universal perspective. These two different perceptions of society and slavery came into contradiction in the early centuries of Christianity, when it was persecuted in the Empire as an illegal religion (Rotman, "Captives and Redeeming Captives"). This required a transformation in the conceptualization of what a society was and what an Empire was. This was needed to allow Church and State to become a single Christian Empire, a process that started with the emperor Constantine (324–337): the legalization of Christianity, his own conversion, the foundation of a new capital, Constantinople ("Constantine's City"), on the site of the ancient Greek Byzantium (modernday Istanbul), and the formal establishment of the Church.

Enslavement and Manumission

Besides their contemporaneous starting points, the Empire and Christianity had something else in common: both presented a universal idea of society. Rome never intended to share the world with political rivals, and Christianity never intended to share the world with rival faiths. This idea of universality was naturally dependent on models of expansion and integration, and slavery played a major role in these. Gaius' first Institute cited above defines the category of enslaved "capitulated aliens" (Latin: *dediticii*) as those "who have in the past taken up arms and fought against the Roman people and then surrendered after defeat." A later Roman legal definition explains that "slaves (*servi*) are so-called because military commanders order their captives to be sold, and so are used to preserve them alive (*servare*) instead of killing them. They are also called *mancipia* because they are seized from the enemy by the strong hand (*manu capiuntur*)" (*The Institutes of Justinian*, bk. 1, tit. 3). This was not the sole method by which someone was enslaved. The same definition stipulates that a man becomes the property of another when born to a female slave (*anchilla*), or by selling himself, provided that he is over twenty years of age.[4]

Of these means of enslavement, war fitted the Empire's social expansion the most. It provided a solution as to what to do with enemies who were not willing to comply with Roman subjugation, by legally incorporating them into Roman society as slaves. At the same time, it made war profitable to both Empire and its soldiers since captives were legitimate

---

4 Buckland, *The Roman Law of Slavery*, 397–436.

Roman booty (see Bradley, "On Captives under the Principate"). To take a typical example: the three Jewish revolts against the Empire in the first and second centuries (66–74, 115–17, 132–35) resulted not only in the total destruction of Jewish life in Judea, Egypt, and Cyprus, but also in a massive supply of new slaves to the slave markets.[5] This had been Roman policy ever since the Roman Republic (the fifth to first centuries BCE). It was applied to political enemies whether they were foreigners or Roman rebels. Enslavement was both a means of punishment and a way to render war and suppression profitable, while war became a good way to enslave enemies and rebels and incorporate them into society as slaves.

Enslavement could be just as easily applied to whoever rebelled against Roman law: convicts who became "slaves of the penalty" (Latin: *servi poenae*).[6] Such convicts lost their status as free persons because of the crimes they committed. Since their life was disposable they were exploited in public enterprises that demanded hard labour: mines, building works, public games. As in the case of captives, it did not matter whether they were of Roman origin or held Roman citizenship. As with captives, the Roman legal system found a way to profit from them instead of executing them. Slaves of the penalty were not private slaves of the emperor and unlike slaves of private owners they were condemned for life and generally could not be manumitted.[7]

Manumission (Latin: *manumissio*) refers to the legal procedure through which slaves were freed and became their own legal entity.[8] Roman manumission created a dependency

---

5 Josephus, *The Jewish War*. Noy, *Jewish Inscriptions*, 1:§26. Rotman, "Captives and Redeeming Captives." Scheidel, "The Roman Slave Supply."

6 J. Burdon, "Slavery as Punishment in Roman Criminal Law," in *Slavery and Other Forms of Unfree Labour*, ed. L. J. Archer (London: Routledge, 1988), 68–85. Buckland, *The Roman Law of Slavery*, 277–78, 403.

7 *Digesta Justiniani*, D.48.19.17; D.48.19.8; Alan Watson, *Roman Slave Law* (Baltimore: Johns Hopkins University Press, 1987).

8 Buckland, *The Roman Law of Slavery*, 449–532.

between manumitted and manumitter and was used to enlarge the family household (see Andreau and Descat, *The Slave in Greece and Rome*). As a freedman (*libertus*) or freedwoman (*liberta*) (from Latin *libertas*, "freedom") the manumitted received the name and civil status of the manumitter (including Roman citizenship if the manumitter was a citizen) and remained attached to the latter's household. We learn about the situation and positions of freedmen from Roman literature, legal acts, and epitaphs.[9] Manumission was used to benefit both the enslaved and the enslaver by profiting from the change of status of the former to that of freedman of the latter. The rationale behind manumission was socio-economic and made it a pivotal institution in Roman society. The manumitted slave gained an independent legal entity, with the right to own property, but remained nonetheless a dependent agent of "the master" (Latin: *dominus*).

Yet, in spite of the centrality of manumission in Roman society, not all Roman slaves were manumitted, but were exploited as a labour force in both rural and urban settings.[10] The economic development of large estates in rural

---

9 W. V. Harris, "Demography, Geography and the Sources of Roman Slaves," *The Journal of Roman Studies* 89 (1999): 62–75. C. Bruun, "Slaves and Freed Slaves," in *The Oxford Handbook of Roman Epigraphy*, ed. C. Bruun and J. Edmondson (Oxford: Oxford University Press, 2014), 605–26. Keith Bradley, *Slavery and Society at Rome* (Cambridge: Cambridge University Press, 1994). Fitzgerald, *Slavery and the Roman Literary Imagination*. Stelios Panayotakis and Michael Paschalis, *Slaves and Masters in the Ancient Novel* (Groningen: Barkhuis, 2019).

10 Attested by the censuses from Aegean and Carian estates: *Inschriften griechischer Städte aus Kleinasien*, vol. 36, part 1, *Die Inschriften von Tralleis und Nysa. Band 1: Die Inschriften von Tralleis*, ed. Fj. B. Poljakov (Bonn: Habelt, 1989) §205. Peter. Thonemann, "Estates and the Land in Late Roman Asia Minor," *Chiron* 37 (2007): 435–78. Also *Inscriptiones graecae*, vol. 12, fasc. 3, *Inscriptiones graecae insularum: Symes, Teutlussae, Teli, Nisyri, Astypalaeae, Anaphes, Therae et Therasiae, Pholegandri, Meli, Cimoli*, ed. F. Hiller (Berlin: Reimer, 1898), §§76–79. G. Kiourtzian, *Recueil*

Italy was depended on enslavement, as was the growth of urban enterprises. Moreover, slavery connected the micro and macro economies in the Empire into a single system. The supply and distribution of enslaved persons functioned on the macro level thanks to political subjugation of internal and external enemies. On the other hand, private economic growth depended on households becoming independent economic enterprises. Acquiring slaves enabled a businessman or a landowner to build a household into a micro economy. Slavery offered an economic tool to the family and helped it expand its supply of food and businesses. In other words, slavery enabled the enslavers to establish themselves as an economic elite better than through other forms of labour, such as wage labourers or tenants (Harper, *Slavery in the Late Roman World*).

The legal status of the enslaved as a human being, albeit classified and managed as thing (Latin: *res*), but someone who could turn into a dependent agent through manumission, provided the enslaver with the ultimate freedom of exploitation. Roman law provided a range of legal procedures (Latin: *peculium, praepositio, servus vicarius*) to enable the owner versatile management and complete control over the enslaved, freedmen, and their labour.[11] This included the possibility of social mobility for an enslaved man who, if found suitable, could advance within the domestic organization, profit from his position as a manager of funds, manage other slaves, be manumitted, and become himself a freedman, a businessman in his own right, and work on his former owner's behalf. The story of the slave Callistus who became bishop of Rome ("pope") in 217 exemplifies this.

---

des inscriptions grecques chretiennes des Cyclades: De la fin du IIIe au VIIe siecle apres J.-C. (Paris: Collège de France, 2000), §142, discussed by Harper, *Slavery in the Late Roman World*, 162–200. Andreau and Descat, *The Slave in Greece and Rome*.

11 Andreau and Descat, *The Slave in Greece and Rome*. Morris Silver, "At the Base of Rome's Peculium Economy," *Fundamina: A Journal of Legal History* 22, no. 1 (2016): 67–93.

Callistus was entrusted by his enslaver ("master") with monetary funds, alms from fellow Christians, to invest. He did not invest the money but gathered other debts through his *peculium* (funds, interests, and debts from his master that he did not own but which he could possess, and manage). He escaped, was caught, brought back, and finally manumitted so that he was able to own things and so pay back his debts. This was not the end of the story. Callistus was arrested while disturbing the reading of Scripture in a synagogue and was sentenced to hard labour in the mines in Sardinia. The emperor Commodus's concubine, a pious Christian, managed to secure the release of a group of Christians enslaved to the mines; Callistus was among them. Appointed by the bishop of Rome Zephyrinus to manage a Christian cemetery, he finally succeeded him as bishop of Rome.[12]

Slavery under the Roman Empire was a combination of absolute Roman private authority (Latin: *patria potestas*) and the opportunity to enlarge it through a constant supply of enslaved persons which Roman military expansion and domination ensured. In other words, slavery provided the nexus between private and public, micro and macro powers. In this it constituted a historical process. This nexus depended on violent, cruel domination which was social, economic, sexual, and psychological in character. Enslavement of children by their parents was not uncommon; indeed, some scholars estimate this to be the main source of slaves within the Roman Empire.[13]

---

12 Hippolytus, *Refutatio omnium haeresium*, ed. Miroslav Marcovich (Berlin: De Gruyter, 1986) / *Refutation of All Heresies*, trans. M. David Litwa (Atlanta: SBL, 2016), bk. 9, ch. 7. Willem Zwalve, "Callistus's Case: Some Legal Aspects of Roman Business Activities," in *The Transformation of Economic Life under the Roman Empire: Proceedings of the Second Workshop of the International Network Impact of Empire*, ed. Lukas de Blois and J. Rich (Leiden: Brill, 2002), 116–27.

13 *Codex Theodosianus* 4.8.6 (pp. 182–83). *Leges Novellae ad Theodosianum Pertinentes*, ed. P. M. Meyer (Berlin: Weidmann, 1962), 138–40. Ville Vuolanto, "Selling a Freeborn Child. Rhetoric and Social Realities in the Late Roman World," *Ancient History* 33 (2003): 169–207.

Sold or offered by their families within the Empire, enslavement of children was frequent, especially in dire economic situations when parents could not provide for their children.

The domination involved in slavery was absolute: the enslaved needed to acknowledge being a disposable property whose very existence was solely in the hand of their enslaver. Yet, enslavement out of self-sale existed, even on a large scale.[14] Selling oneself into slavery could provide a means for poor people in dire circumstances within the Empire to escape their status as taxpayers or from their debts, become enslaved under terms of individual indenturing contracts, and use the internal Roman slave market to migrate to Italy and become integrated as enslaved, and later become a freedman of the Roman elite. This was the story of Trimalchio, a first-century literary character in Petronius' *Satyricon*. He sold himself to evade his taxes and debts in order to advance himself and become rich. He became a manager in his enslaver's household, inherited from him, and became a wealthy Roman citizen.

Slavery was therefore a tool for social mobility: on the one hand, enslaving of captives, rebels, and convicts suppressed their ability to act as free persons. On the other hand, enslavement was also used as a way to climb the social ladder by becoming the enslaved of a rich and powerful enslaver. This was considered a high position in itself. Despite its special socioeconomic role, slavery was not the only form of domination in Roman society, and not the only mode of exploitation. It was not even the major one. It always coexisted with other forms of wage labour and land tenure.[15]

---

14 Harris, "Demography, Geography and the Sources of Roman Slaves." Morris Silver, "The Role of Slave Markets in Migration from the Near East to Rome," *Klio* 98, no. 1 (2016): 184–202. Jacques Ramin and Paul Veyne, "Droit romain et société: les hommes libres qui passent pour esclaves et l'esclavage volontaire," *Historia* 30 (1981): 472–97.

15 Koenraad Verboven and Christian Laes, eds., *Work, Labour, and Professions in the Roman World* (Leiden: Brill, 2017). Peter Temin,

Its main advantage, the one that gave it its central role, was the combination between how it could be managed in a versatile way whilst allowing extreme forms of violent control. Slavery became especially useful in forming an imperial elite. It allowed you to enter the public imperial authority. In this it could become profitable, although in different ways, to both enslaver and enslaved. It provided the former with the means to become financially independent and powerful, while the latter depended on this advancement.

Was the Roman Empire a Slave Society?

Scholars estimate the number of slaves in the Roman Empire to be between ten and twenty percent of the entire population, while estimates for Italy and the city of Rome can go as high as thirty to forty percent.[16] These estimates are mainly based on modern demographic models and sporadic descriptions in Roman sources, and not on historical registers. If we use epigraphic evidence, over twenty-seven thousand persons have been identified in inscriptions from the city of Rome (both the Republic and Empire) as either slaves or freedmen.[17] The distinction between the two is difficult to establish unless explicitly mentioned. This contradicts the common view of Roman society in which the enslaved constituted a large stratum. Conversely, according to Galen (ca. 130–210), in the second-century city of Pergamum (near Bergama in today's western Turkey) the number of slaves equalled that of male citizens and that of women citizens,

---

"The Labor Market of the Early Roman Empire," *The Journal of Interdisciplinary History* 34, no. 4 (2004): 513–38.

16 Andreau and Descat, *The Slave in Greece and Rome*, 46–52. Walter Scheidel, "The Slave Population of Roman Italy: Speculations and Constraints," *Topoi* 9 (1999): 129–44. Scheidel, "The Roman Slave Supply."

17 Heikki Solin, *Die stadtrömischen Sklavennamen*, vol. 3, *Barbarische Namen. Indices* (Stuttgart: Steiner, 1996). Bruun, "Slaves and Freed Slaves."

namely forty thousand.[18] This is an enormous proportion of the urban population. But we cannot extrapolate from this across the entire Empire. More generally we might ask whether quantity and percentages are good criteria to determine what a slave society is.

The term "slave societies" is used by historians to group together the ancient societies of Greece and Rome with modern Brazil, the Caribbean, and the antebellum South in the United States in opposition to "societies with slaves."[19] This concept sees slavery as the major means of production in a stratified economic model that separated enslaving proprietors from enslaved labourers. Yet, in the Roman Empire slavery was not used to create an economically stratified model. The enslaved were legally distinguished from other members of society, but they did not have a distinct economic role or socioeconomic position. Others, hired free born or freedmen, filled the same economic roles. If slaves are often considered the main rural labour force in Italy, this was in no way the case in other parts of the Empire. Egyptian villages in the Empire, for example, were composed of small-scale landowners for whom possessing one to four slaves was common.[20] The spread of slavery was not uniform. Slaves were used in all possible socioeco-

---

18 Galen, *De propriorum animi [...]*, ed. Wilko de Boer (Leipzig: Teubner, 1937), ch. 9.

19 Keith Hopkins, *Conquerors and Slaves* (Cambridge: Cambridge University Press, 1978). M. I. Finley, *Ancient Slavery and Modern Ideology* (London: Chatto & Windus, 1980) and Finley, *Classical Slavery* (London: Cass, 1986).

20 Roger Bagnall, "Landholding in Late Roman Egypt: The Distribution of Wealth," *The Journal of Roman Studies* 82 (1992): 128–49 and Bagnall, "Slavery and Society in Late Roman Egypt," in *Law, Politics and Society in the Ancient Mediterranean World*, ed. B. Halpern and D. W. Hobson (Sheffield: Sheffield Academic Press, 1993), 220–38. Jean A. Straus, "Liste commentée des contrats de vente d'esclaves passés en Égypte aux époques grecque, romaine et byzantine," *Zeitschrift für Papyrologie und Epigraphik* 131 (2000): 135–44. Iza Biezunska-Malowist, *L'esclavage dans l'Égypte gréco-romaine*, trans. J. Wolf, vol. 2, *Période romaine* (Wrocław: Nauk, 1977).

nomic roles, but not exclusively. The socioeconomic position of a slave of a rich person who had climbed high as manager in the urban household had nothing in common with a person who was condemned to the mines, or a person enslaved in an Egyptian village, though all three shared the same legal status. Slaves could well be found on a higher socioeconomic plane in comparison to other freeborn persons thanks to the organizational position they held in their owner's household. The enslaver determined the socioeconomic position of the enslaved. But the legal status of the enslaved allowed the use of severe forms of control for various forms of exploitation.

Much more than through employment of other forms of labour, the acquisition, exploitation, and control of slaves provided the enslaver with the ability to develop and maintain socioeconomic independence. It ensured an exploitation which was based on complete socioeconomic dependency and personal control. In this it formed a part of the Roman system of kinship. Freeborn family members before their emancipation (Latin: *emancipatio*)—the legal process through which a person acquired his own legal rights (Latin: *sui juris*)—were under the complete control and domination of the *pater familias* (the family's head/father). Roman slavery gave the *pater familias* the means to enlarge his authority and socioeconomic independence through human property. The question is whether this qualifies Rome as a "slave society."

Let's consider a supposedly typical slave society: the antebellum US South. According to the 1860 national census, slaves formed a population of 3,950,511 out of a total of 12,240,293 in the states where slavery was legal.[21] However the American South was not a separate country within the USA. The economy in the northern states profited indirectly from slavery in the South.[22] Slaves made up 32.27% of the

---

21 https://faculty.weber.edu/kmackay/statistics_on_slavery. htm based on https://www.census.gov/library/publications/1864/ dec/1860a.html (accessed November 10, 2020).

22 Sven Beckert and Seth Rockman, *Slavery's Capitalism: A New History of American Economic Development* (Philadelphia: University

population in the South, but 12.56% of the entire US population (31,443,321). In the same way, the Caribbean colonies and Brazil cannot be termed slave societies. Eleven million trafficked enslaved Africans survived the transatlantic slave trade between the fifteenth and nineteenth centuries (and over two million died en route: Eltis, *The Rise of African Slavery in the Americas*). They formed a substantial part of the population of the Americas, but they did not constitute a high percentage of the entire colonial societies which included the local population of the colonies and the populations in the mother countries. If we consider the US South, Brazil, and the Caribbean as independent societies, we might conclude that they were slave societies, since their economy was largely based on enslaved labour. However, these were not independent economies, but constituted part of larger societies in which slavery was by no means the majority of the labour force. The colonies were an engine of economic growth for both the colonial elite and the royal authorities of the entire colonial structure. It helped create a new socioeconomic elite and benefited the mother countries.

Though the enslavement of human beings may not constitute the major form of exploitation in a given society, it can still provide the enslavers with an exclusive means to enlarge their own business to the benefit of the state and their position in it. This is what is characteristic of slavery: it holds a unique place in the dynamics between the private (enslaving owners) and the public (enslaving public authority). The public authority provides private forces the means and opportunities to enslave others in order to enlarge and manage their socioeconomic independence and wealth. When the latter act with the former and on their behalf, slavery thrives. When

---

of Pennsylvania Press, 2016). Gavin Wright, *Slavery and American Economic Development* (Baton Rouge: Louisiana State University Press, 2006). Edward E. Baptist, *The Half Has Never Been Told: Slavery and the Making of American Capitalism* (New York: Basic, 2014). Bonnie Martin, "Slavery's Invisible Engine: Mortgaging Human Property," *The Journal of Southern History* 76, no. 4 (2010): 817–66.

public and private forces find themselves in conflict, the first will attempt to limit the second and their means to enlarge their power by using slavery. In this way slavery is part of the social relationships between the private and the public. It operates and is controlled through its *de jure* (public) definition and *de facto* (private) reality.

The dynamics of power relations within Roman society between public and private, which slavery facilitated, changed dramatically in the late Roman Empire due to two key reforms: the adoption of Christianity by Constantine and the reform in the status of private property. Slavery depended on the definition of what was private and public and the way it functioned in Roman society, and influenced the dynamics between private and public power in the Empire.

Assimilation of Church and State

We have previously seen that Paul paved the way for the idea of a virtual Christian society under One Christ, in which slavery, ownership, and gender were not supposed to be an issue. Slaves were not excluded from the Church and were baptized as part of the household under the initiative of its head. Slavery was a secular matter. So preachers who allegedly provoked slaves to become Christians and flee their pagan owners were condemned.[23]

The Stoic Roman philosopher Seneca (ca. 4 BC–65 CE), Paul's contemporary, had defined slavery as a human condition which does not determine the person's better part, his free mind. His follower, Epictetus (50–135 CE), himself a manumitted slave, developed the idea that slavery and freedom are matters of the mind, independent of one's actual state of being under the domination of someone else.[24] Freedom for

---

23 *Adversus Marcione*, in Tertullian, *Opera, I*, ed. A. Kroymann, Corpus christianorum series latina 1 (Turnhout: Brepols, 1954). Available online in Patrologia Latina 2 and www.thelatinlibrary.com/tertullian/tertullian.marcionem.shtml.

24 Epictetus, *The Discourses as Reported by Arrian*, ed. and trans.

Epictetus was the ability to decide between what is right and wrong. Although the enslaver's dominion over the enslaved body is absolute, the enslaved mind can remain free once it adopts an indifference towards the body. Christian thinkers developed an equivalent perspective that distinguished slavery of the body and of the mind. This prevented any development of abolitionist views. Nevertheless, the new notion of a single comprehensive and global Christian society was innovative as was the idea of a class-based earthly society in opposition to an undifferentiated spiritual organization. Joining both notions together played a decisive role in developing a new society for the Byzantine Empire.

Since Constantine's legalization of Christianity and his formal establishment of the Church, slavery, as other juridical Roman institutions, attracted more and more attention from Christian thinkers: the homilies of John Chrysostom (349–407), the writings of the three Cappadocian Church Fathers of the fourth century, and then Ambrose (ca. 340–397) and Augustine (354–430) all write about slavery (Garnsey, *Ideas of Slavery from Aristotle to Augustine*). These thinkers lived in regions where slavery was omnipresent in both urban and rural settings. Most of them addressed the subject of slavery and developed Christian justifications for its existence.[25] According to John Chrysostom, in creating man God made him not a slave but free; sin, war, and greed made man a slave.[26] Like him Ambrose and Augustine maintained that

---

W. A. Oldfather, 2 vols. (Cambridge, MA: Harvard University Press, 1928), bk. 4, ch. 1. C. Edwards, "Free Yourself! Slavery, Freedom and the Self in Seneca's Letters," in *Seneca and the Self*, ed. S. Bartsch and D. Wray (Cambridge: Cambridge University Press, 2009), 139–59. R. S. Braicovich, "Freedom and Determinism in Epictetus' Discourses," *Classical Quarterly* 60, no. 1 (2010): 202–20.

25 Garnsey, *Ideas of Slavery from Aristotle to Augustine*. Glancy, *Slavery in Early Christianity*. De Wet, *The Unbound God*.

26 From homily 22 in John Chrysostom, *Homiliae XXIV in Epistolam ad Ephesios*, in his *Opera omnia*, ed. J.-P. Migne, Patrologia Graeca 62 (Paris: Migne, 1857–1866), 155–61 (available online). Chris L.

slavery was not a condition of "nature" (Latin: *natura*), but the consequence of foolishness (Ambrose) or sin (Augustine). Unlike Aristotle, they used the term "nature" to signify the laws created by God. Slavery was not an essential part of man's existence but a just punishment for his sins and character. It had a moral Christian justification.

This Christian justification corresponded to contemporary laws of the Empire by which war and not nature created slavery.[27] Both war and sin were human actions that made enslavement a justified moral punishment of the enslaved who was thus considered a criminal, not a victim. Christianity as an official religion did not challenge the Empire's recognition of slavery and its means of enslavement. On the contrary, it provided a moral justification for its existence. Slave owners were not encouraged to manumit their slaves. Believers who became monks and wished to manumit their slaves did so to free themselves from their earthly possessions, not out of compassion.[28] This overlap between Church and Empire had therefore two aspects. On the one hand, it provided the Empire with a notion of one universal religious society sharing a spiritual destiny regardless of legal and socioeconomic categories. On the other hand, it gave the Church the moral justification to participate in the power game that enslavement generated between private and public notions of property.

Private and Public Notions of Property

Some Christian ascetics had other views and denounced the inequality that possession entailed. Property, including human property which was incompatible with the ascetic

---

de Wet, "John Chrysostom on Slavery: The Status Quaestionis," *Journal of Early Christian History* 4, no. 2 (2014): 31–39.

27 *The Institutes of Justinian*, bk. 1, tit. 3.

28 *Vie de Sainte Mélanie*, ed. D. Gorce (Paris: Cerf, 1962), chs. 9–11. *Vie de Syméon le Fou et Vie de Jean de Chypre*, ed. A.-J. Festugière and L. Rydén (Paris: Geuthner 1974), 124–25.

way.[29] In the fourth century Gregory of Nyssa (335–394) addressed the question of slavery by challenging the idea of human beings as property: "So, when someone turns the property of God into his own property, and arrogates dominion to his own kind, so as to think himself the owner of men and women [...], what is he doing but overstepping his own nature through pride, regarding himself as something different from his subordinates?"[30] Slavery was therefore a wrongful human exploitation of God's authority bestowed on man since it appropriated God's concept of property to man's own benefit. When men subordinate God's property and make it their own, they commit a sin in depriving God of his property: man. Contrary to other Church writers and Christian ascetics who wrote against earthly possessions, Gregory of Nyssa was an advocate for manumission and preached in its favour in the 370s and 380s. At that period bishops had received from the secular authorities the power to enact manumissions in the Church (Latin: *manumissio in ecclesia*). Unlike his contemporary John Chrysostom who exhorted slaveholders to manumit their slaves out of compassion and philanthropy, Gregory of Nyssa developed a firm view against slavery as offending God's authority. Although we can read this as a new Christian doctrine, even abolitionist in direction, at its core Gregory of Nyssa's idea was based on a perspective that rejected some convenient separation between a spiritual and a corporeal society and between public and private. According to him there could be only one master, God, who is the sole owner of humanity.

Gregory of Nyssa's approach is reflected in the religious language that was developed by Christian writers who adopted from Judaism the term "the master" for the one God (Greek: *ho kurios/despotēs*, Latin: *dominus*, Hebrew: *adon*, or English:

---

29 Ilaria Ramelli, *Social Justice and the Legitimacy of Slavery. The Role of Philosophical Asceticism from Ancient Judaism to Late Antiquity* (Oxford: Oxford University Press, 2016).

30 Gregory of Nyssa, *Homily on Ecclesiastes*, translated in de Wet, *The Unbound God*, 6.

"the Lord"). This metaphor fitted very well the concept that Christianity took from Judaism of the one God who was the owner, the master, and the proprietor of the entire universe. If God was THE master, then the believer was his slave. Indeed, Christian believers started to refer to themselves as "the slave of God" (Greek: *ho doulos tou theou*). This had not only a metaphorical meaning, but reflected a new perspective of society and empire, and the place Christianity and the Church held in it. The believer was perceived firstly as God's subject. All service and loyalty (Greek: *douleia*, Latin: *servitium*) were duties directed firstly towards Him. To be a slave acquired a new social meaning: being in the eternal service and subordination of a master; they were to be his subjects. This change of social mentality was one of the most important impacts that the idea of slavery had on the monotheistic turn. Its roots are to be found in the book of Exodus, where God is designated as the owner and master of the people of Israel since he had redeemed them from their earthly slavery in Egypt.

During the second- and third-century Roman persecutions of Christians this idea of religious slavery gave a moral justification to disobeying the emperor's command and worship by those who considered themselves God's slaves. Christian authors presented themselves as martyrs, going happily to their torture and execution.[31] Like Roman slaves who were tortured to prove their master's innocence, tortured Christians were fulfilling their obligations in being a part of the body of their one-and-only master, owner, and enslaver in heaven. Their torments and execution testified to their faith and to his innocence. Perceiving themselves as God's slaves, their duty was to fulfill the service and duties that their position entailed. In other words: they were embodying what Gregory of Nyssa later articulated in the fourth century: there is only one legitimate owner of human beings.

The new language that Christianity introduced about slavery and its innovative views on ownership had concrete

---

31 For a characteristic of martyrologies, see H. Musurillo, *Acts of the Christian Martyrs* (Oxford: Clarendon Press, 2000).

expression following the reforms that the emperor Diocletian (284–305) introduced to the fiscal system on landed property. Diocletian's reforms subjugated all landed property to the public authority and made it liable to tax. No private property henceforth existed independently of state authority. The public authorities developed a system of control to implement its authority over the property owner. Theoretically the reform introduced a new notion of private property: it was no longer completely private, but became subordinated to the imperial authority which controlled it and benefited from it. Gregory of Nyssa echoes this perspective in declaring that there is no private property apart from God's property. Naturally, he was speaking not of land but of human beings. But there too, major changes occurred in the relationship between the enslaving proprietor and enslaved human property, which enabled the intervention of the emperor's authority in the private relationship between enslaver and enslaved.

The unlimited power of the father as head of the family (Latin: *patria potestas*) over the bodies and lives of his subordinated, whether slaves or children, was an ancient Roman practice.[32] From the first century CE onwards, Roman legislators intervened more and more in relationships considered to be under the private authority, and always in one direction: limiting the private power of private owners. To take one typical example, in 294 the imperial authority forbade the enslavement and selling of children except in special circumstances.[33] What had been under the sole authority of the father and considered to be beyond public authority became, from the fourth century, a matter of law. Enslaving and procuring of one's own children became illegal. In a similar way to Diocletian's reforms on landed property, the impe-

---

32 Yan Thomas, "Vitae necisque potestas. Le père, la cité, la mort," in *Du châtiment dans la cité. Supplices corporels et peine de mort dans le monde antique. Table ronde organisée par l'EFR avec le concours du Centre national de la recherche scientifique (Rome 9–11 novembre, 1982)* (Rome: Ecole française de Rome, 1984), 499–548.

33 *Codex Justinianus*, C.4.43.

rial power intervened in matters of private authority, limited it, and turned it into a matter for the authorities. Enslavement now depended on a tripartite relationship: emperor–enslaver–enslaved.

To implement these new dynamics between the public and private authority, the Empire used a new concept of slavery: slaves gained civil status, a special status within society, that is the *civitas* or Empire. Though they were a type of property they were not just chattel. The law intervened in the way this type of property was defined, used, and controlled, and it also manipulated the processes of their manumission. Slaves, just like children, women, foreigners, and freedmen, had a particular legal status which determined their condition. Changing the legal definition of slavery was used to redefine the relationship between public and private authority. Exploitation was a way to increase private authority. But this exploitation was defined, supervised, and controlled by the public authority for its own benefit. The case of castrated slaves exemplifies this.

Castration of men had been prohibited under Roman law since the first century. The penalty for breaking this prohibition became harsher and harsher. In a case of violation, Roman law gave the enslaved the exceptional right to denounce his enslaver.[34] This did not prevent the use in the Empire of eunuchs, who were considered exotic and expensive merchandise.[35] Castrated slaves were mainly the property of very rich slaveholders (their prices were fifty *solidi* in comparison to twenty *solidi*, and thirty instead of ten for boys).[36] Yet, since the fourth century the imperial authority took legislative means to restrict private ownership of castrated slaves by confiscating them for imperial use.[37] From

---

34 *Digesta Justiniani*, D.48.8.4; Watson, *Roman Slave Law*, 63 and 128

35 Youval Rotman, "The Paradox of Roman Eunuchism: A Juridical Historical Approach," *Scripta Classica Israelica* 34 (2015): 129–50.

36 *Codex Justinianus*, C.6.43.3.1; C.7.7.1.5.

37 *Codex Justinianus*, C.12.5.4.1; C.4.42.2.

the fifth century onwards eunuchs were enslaved only for the use of the imperial palace where they performed an elaborate array of special functions. Many of them were manumitted, rose very high, and became personal attendants of the emperor and bearers of political and top military positions. Two examples were Eutropius who was the counsel of emperor Arcadius (395–408) and Narses (478–573) who was the chief general of Justinian (527–565). Both were castrated and enslaved in their childhood and became influential in the imperial court in Constantinople.[38] By changing the law the imperial authority manipulated the private possession of slaves to its benefit which, in the case of eunuchs, created an imperial monopoly.

Conclusion

Slavery as a system and the forms of enslavement which composed it were used in the Roman Empire to alter the dynamics between the private and the public. Managing an Empire demanded a new elite for whom forms of enslavement were legalized and defined by the state. At the same time Christianity, which was both a religious and a political movement, introduced new concepts of society and authority. If Gregory of Nyssa advanced in the fourth century the idea that all humans were the property of the one God, the logic follows that the emperor, now acting since that same century as God's representative on earth, had the authority to manage and apply God's authority by changing definitions of human property and public property.

The assimilation of Church and state was a process of several centuries during which the latter became an incarnation of the Christian notion of a society of believers. The state used the Church as a vector of its authority, and exploited it to accumulate, subordinate, and dominate the authority of private slaveholders over their dependents. The adaptable

---

38 Claudius Claudianus, *Œuvres*, ed. and trans. J.-L. Charlet, 3 vols. in 2 (Paris: Belles lettres, 1991) 1:48–49. Procopius, *De bello Gothico*.

character of slavery and the versatile roles it could play made it a tool in the development of society and imperial authority as it moved from the Roman to the Byzantine state. The innovative model of society and empire in Byzantium was copied, adapted, and developed by the new medieval political entities in the period that followed.

Thus the importance of slavery lies not only in the place it holds in the economic organization of a particular society, but in the way it is used as a system in forming and changing social and political dynamics. In this slavery functions as a historical process. This becomes evident when analyzing the roles slavery played in the developing medieval world. In the next chapter we will follow the evolution of the historical process of slavery in a period of transformation that resulted in multiple monotheistic civilizations.

Chapter 3

Enslavement, Captivity, and the Monotheistic Turn

FIFTH TO SEVENTH CENTURIES

Ever since Roman slavery became a focus of research it has been treated under two axiomatic theses that became inseparable. The first was that slaves formed a social class of Roman society and played a major role in the economic life of the Empire. The second was that Roman slavery declined along with the declne of the Empire. The two theses together have determined the way we define and understand what Roman and medieval slaveries were. So, it is essential to analyze this idea of decline in the state of slavery in the passage from Late Antiquity into the Middle Ages.

Upon his death in 395 the emperor Theodosius (347–395) left both his sons as co-emperors of the Empire: Arcadius (395–408) reigned from Constantinople and Honorius (395–423) from Rome. The Roman ruling authority, the *imperium* (i.e., Empire) was shared between the two but was divided geographically: the first ruled the Greek-speaking Eastern parts of the Empire, and the second the Latin West. The Empire's unity was kept, and any decision of either applied to the entire Empire. And yet, this political change was the beginning of a long process that transformed the unified Roman Empire into a medieval world of distinct civilizations. The Roman Empire continued to rule the northeastern regions of the Mediterranean. Today we term it "Byzantium," the ancient Greek name of the Empire's new capital Constantinople (namely Istanbul, Europe's largest city today). The city's inhabitants named themselves "Byzantines," a term we apply nowadays to the entire population of the Eastern Roman Empire whose language was Greek and whose religion was Orthodox Christianity (though they themselves still saw themselves as *Rhōmaioi* or Romans). Unlike the period of the first to fourth centuries, it no longer ruled the Mediterranean alone.

Meanwhile, in the West newcomers of Germanic and Asian origin appeared. They founded new political entities within the Western borders of the Empire: the kingdoms of the Vandals, the Visigoths, the Franks, and the Ostrogoths. In the sixth century Justinian (527–565) launched extensive and successful military campaigns to regain all these territories. His victories were short lived and were overshadowed by the conquest of the Byzantine East in the seventh century by the Sassanian Empire, a Persian Zoroastrian state that ruled over what is today Iran and Iraq between 224 and 651. What was lost was later reconquered by the emperor Herakalios (610–641), only to be lost again, and this time definitively, to a new rival: the Muslim Arabs.

From this period of wide-ranging geopolitical changes a stable new picture appeared in the eighth century. The territories of the Roman Empire were now divided between three political blocks: Byzantium in the northeast and central Mediterranean, the Carolingian empire in western and central Europe and in the south and east the Muslim Caliphate that extended from Iberia to Persia. This new medieval map was also a religious map. Although all three were monotheistic, the three blocks had different faiths, different religious institutions, different cultures and languages, different socioeconomic systems and legal institutions, all of which made them distinct civilizations. Spread across these three, Jewish communities formed a fourth monotheistic civilization with its own religious, legal, and social institutions.

The formation of this medieval map has traditionally been viewed as a decline of Roman structures by historians who needed to analyze what went wrong, why these newcomers, whether Germanic, Persian, or Arabian, could not be held back. The idea of decline was not confined to the

Roman Empire. Modern scholarship has treated Byzantium similarly, perceiving it as a declining empire in spite of the fact that it held firm, almost without interruption, for more than a millennium (324–1453), longer than any other Mediterranean civilization. Naturally, the notion of decline carries a moral judgment: why, for example, not consider this as a time of vigorous innovations in politics, culture, religion, and thought? Indeed, the period from the third to seventh centuries, called "Late Antiquity" is perceived today as such.

And yet, the idea of decline has not disappeared, and has become entangled with the idea of other declines, amongst which that of slavery. If the expansion of the Roman Empire and the Roman economy were tightly connected to the place that slavery played in both, then their decline must also have been connected to a decline of slavery. This perspective is indirectly linked to Marx's definition of slavery as a mode of production and to a historical determinism according to which the form of exploitation that determines the mode of production changes from one historical period to another.

Whether we define slavery as a mode of production or not, we cannot accept today the thesis that it was the most characteristic mode of production in Antiquity, nor the idea that every new age sees the rise of new modes of production and new forms of exploitation. In a deterministic Marxist perspective a historical age is defined by its distinct modes of exploitation and a struggle over the means of production. The idea of a decline of slavery then gets linked to concepts of "slave societies" versus "societies with slaves" (see chapter 2 above). If the Roman Empire was indeed a "slave society," i.e., one built primarily on exploitation of slaves, its decline must logically denote a decline in the use of slaves. The fact that slavery existed in Antiquity along with other forms of exploitation, the fact that slavery and enslavement continued to be part of all medieval societies, and the fact that enslaved people played a role in medieval social and economic life invite us to reexamine the relation between historical development and slavery.

Humanity in Periods of Uncertainty (Poverty, Natural Disasters)

Late Antiquity was a period of great innovation in the fields of thought, religion, culture, and economic expansion. And yet the period of the fifth to seventh centuries witnessed major crises which affected both its demography and economy. Firstly, the continuous invasions that started in the fourth century were accompanied by urban and rural changes and resulted in the settlement of new forces across large parts of the Roman Empire: the Vandals in North Africa, the Visigoths in Iberia, the Franks in Gaul, the Ostrogoths and later the Lombards in Italy, the Anglo-Saxons in Britain, the Huns and the Avars in the Danube plain, the Slavs in the Balkans. These mass movements were accompanied with ongoing wars. Take the case of Britain for example: the withdrawal of the Romans in the early fifth century and the migration and settlement of the Anglo-Saxons started a period of armed conflict between neighbouring kingdoms or chiefdoms, whose elite was formed out of tribal leaders, either native Celtic ones or Anglo-Saxon migrants. These conflicts led to the enslavement of people captured in raids, as well as tribute and extortion, integral to these inter-tribal and inter-chiefdom struggles (Pelteret, *Slavery in Early Mediaeval England*). Here too, we need to consider enslavement not only as the result of the political situation, but also as its objective: a way to increase the power of the tribe, the chieftain, or the king.

Climate catastrophes of the mid-sixth century also had major demographic and economic consequences. A volcanic eruption in Iceland in 536 created a fog over Europe and the wider Mediterranean and a long cold period there in the years following.[1] In Italy in particular the sixth century expe-

---

[1] U. Büntgen et al. "Cooling and Societal Change during the Late Antique Little Ice Age from 536 to around 660 AD," *Nature Geoscience* 9, no. 3 (2016): 231–36. M. Sigl et al., "Timing and Climate Forcing of Volcanic Eruptions for the Past 2,500 Years," *Nature* 523 (2015): 543–49.

rienced extreme rainfall and increased flooding.[2] In 541–542 the bubonic plague spread rapidly from Egypt causing major depopulations from time to time across the Eastern Mediterranean.[3] Notwithstanding these destabilizing phenomena, Justinian's reign (527–565) was marked by military success and great cultural and intellectual output. How can we account for what seems like two contradictory states of the same Empire, and how is slavery connected to it? Was this a period of socioeconomic decline, and was slavery a part of this decline?

Documents of various types—legislative, literary, documentary—from different parts of the Empire in this period show that despite the precarious economic situation, slavery did not disappear. Quite the contrary: the merchandising of people became more frequent, in particular enslaved freeborn persons. Several papyri from Egypt attest to increased kidnapping and enslaving of freeborn inhabitants for their economic value.[4] Cases of parents in dire financial straits who

---

2 Giovanni Zanchetta et al., "Beyond One-Way Determinism: San Frediano's Miracle and Climate Change in Central and Northern Italy in Late Antiquity," *Climatic Change* 165, no. 25 (2021): https://doi.org/10.1007/s10584-021-03043-x.

3 The scale of destruction is a matter of debate: Dionysius Ch. Stathakopoulos, *Famine and Pestilence in the Late Roman and Early Byzantine Empire: A Systematic Survey of Subsistence Crises and Epidemics* (London: Routledge, 2004). Peter Sarris, "The Justinianic Plague: Origins and Effects," *Continuity and Change* 17, no. 2 (2002): 169–82. Lester K. Little, *Plague and the End of Antiquity: The Pandemic of 541–750* (New York: Cambridge University Press, 2007). M. Eisenberg and L. Mordechai, "The Justinianic Plague: An Interdisciplinary Review," *Byzantine and Modern Greek Studies* 43, no. 2 (2019): 156–80. L. Mordechai and M. Eisenberg, "Rejecting Catastrophe: The Case of the Justinianic Plague," *Past and Present* 244, no. 1 (2018): 3–50.

4 SB 18:13173 and SB 3:6097 (catalogued in *Sammelbuch griechischer Urkunden aus Ägypten*, ed. Friedrich Preisigke et al., 27 vols. to date (Strasbourg: Trübner 1915–)). P.Cair. Masp. 1:67089 and P.Cair. Masp. 3:67204 (cataloged fully by volume and item in Maspero, *Papyrus grecs d'époque byzantine*).

offered up or sold their children were known and legalized. Creditors would take away the children of their debtors and enslave them as collateral.[5] Augustine's letter about the raids of slave traders attests to the same phenomenon in North Africa.[6] In 528 Cassiodorus describes the annual fair in south Italy on St. Cyprian's day and writes about peasants from the countryside who came to sell their sons and daughters, while Gregory the Great mentions enslavement resulting from the financial effects of the plague.[7] Raids were a common phenomenon, and the story of St. Patrick, himself kidnapped from his home in Britain in the fifth century and enslaved in Ireland, was not unique. It is reflected in the literature of the period, for example in Jerome's *The Life of Malchus the Captive.*

This does not point to a decline but, on the contrary, to new forms of enslavement and enslaving, legal and illegal, of the freeborn. Other descriptions of dire economic situations attest to cases of enslavement of free children as well as kidnapping and prostituting of freeborn girls.[8] Enslavement became a means of survival for the poor. Harsh economic conditions pushed people more and more towards exploiting other people, including their own children or their own selves.[9] Poverty is often forgotten in the historical analysis of slavery, in contrast to its place in the scholarship of modern slavery. In precarious economic situations it acquires a cru-

---

5 *Novellae Justiniani*, 134.7; P.Lond. 6:1915.

6 Augustine, *Epistolae ex duobus codicibus nuper in lucem prolatae*, ed. Johannes Divjak, Corpus scriptorum ecclesiasticorum latinorum 88 (Vienna: Hoelder–Pichler–Tempsky, 1981), Epistle 10*.

7 Cassiodorus, *Variae*, ed. Theodore Mommsen, MGH Auct. ant. 12 (Berlin: Weidmann, 1894), bk. 8, chap. 33. Gregory the Great, *Registrum epistularum*, bk 9, no. 232. Thomas MacMaster, "The Transformative Impact of the Slave Trade on the Roman World, 580–720" (PhD diss., University of Edinburgh, 2016), 61.

8 *Novellae Justiniani*, 14.

9 *Concilia aevi Merovingici*, ed. F. Maassen, MGH Conc. 1. (Hanover: Hahn, 1893), 195. Alice Rio, "Self-Sale and Voluntary Entry into Unfreedom, 300–1100," *Journal of Social History*, 45, no. 3 (2012): 661–85.

cial role in providing the conditions and rationale for enslavement. In the fifth to seventh centuries it became particularly dominant. This was not the "voluntary poverty" that the Church proclaimed, which was mostly directed to the rich, but an extreme form of economic poverty that threatened to completely destroy the lives of less fortunate families. For them enslavement presented a means of survival.[10]

Commodifying people and their labour might be a response to economic difficulties for poor families, but it required a demand for slaves. The market for human merchandise did not decline. Prosperous households continued to enslave people who were kidnapped, sold by their kin or by themselves. The private household economy in both rural and urban environments depended on enslavement. Slaves worked in the grain-exporting areas of Africa, Sicily, and Sardinia and in commercial stock rearing.[11] In Italy slaves appeared in land registers alongside labourers of other statuses. Papyri from Egypt and travel descriptions by Cosmas Indicopleustes reveal the slave trade persisting in Egypt in the sixth century. Kidnapped, offered up, or sold by their parents, girls and boys were enslaved in North Africa, Britain, France, and Italy. We find descriptions by Pope Gregory the Great (ca. 540–604), Gregory of Tours (ca. 538–594), and Bede (673–735) of the slave trade in the sixth and seventh centuries, including children going from Britain to Gaul and Rome.[12] All this points to a widespread trend from freeborn status into enslavement.

---

10 Evelyne Patlagean, *Pauvreté économique et pauvreté sociale à Byzance, 4e–7e siècles* (Paris: Mouton, 1977).

11 *Codex Theodosianus* 2.25.1 and 9.31. Cf. Sidonius Apollinaris, *Poems and Letters*, ed. W. B. Anderson (London: Heinemann, 1963) epist. 2.2. MacMaster, "The Transformative Impact," 61.

12 Gregory the Great, *Registrum epistularum*, bk. 3, no. 37; bk. 6, no. 10. Gregory of Tours, *History of the Franks*, bk. 7, ch. 45 (available online at https://sourcebooks.fordham.edu/basis/gregory-hist.asp). Bede, *Ecclesiastical History of the English People*, ed. B. Colgrave and R. A. B. Mynors (Oxford: Oxford University Press, 1992), bk. 2, ch. 1. David Pelteret, "Slave Raiding and Slave Trading in Early

The fact that no decline is visible in the use of slaves in either Italy or Egypt, despite the economic and climatic challenges of the period, reveals the dynamic and adaptable character of slavery: the type of enslavement changes in light of the economic circumstances. Economic insecurity and demographic changes stimulated enslavement and changes in one's legal status. As slave raids and the enslavement of freeborn children became common anyone could become kidnapped and enslaved; those who had means could be ransomed by their kin. The state which defined such acts of kidnapping and enslavement as illegal was apparently unable to protect its inhabitants. In Christianity, Judaism, and Islam protection from enslavement became a matter for the religious community.

The Religious Society: Captivity, Enslavement, Ransom

Although we commonly use the terms "religious community" or "community of believers" we can better understand them as newly formed societies with their own legal codes, as social and political organizations built around a shared sense of religious belonging. In Rabbinic Judaism and early Christianity this religious sentiment was translated into a sense of religious solidarity. The religious community became responsible for the ransoming of enslaved believers. Both Rabbinic Judaism and early Christianity simultaneously developed the precept of redeeming fellow believers who had been captured, kidnapped, and enslaved, and special funds and monetary collections were set aside to this end (Rotman, "Captives and Redeeming Captives"). This practice is attested in theological writings, religious law such as the Talmud, and wills of Christians who left their property to redeem enslaved fellow Christians.[13] Religious solidarity was applied also in cases of

---

England," *Anglo-Saxon England* 9 (1980): 99–114. Pelteret, *Slavery in Early Mediaeval England*. MacMaster, "The Transformative Impact."

13 Ambrose of Milan, *De officiis / Les devoirs*, vol. 2: *Livres II–III*, ed. Maurice Testard (Paris: Belles lettres, 1992), 2.xv.70–71 and

enslaved children and women who had no financial means to ransom themselves.[14]

A precarious world that led to a precarious civil status was met by a new solidarity: the society of believers. No Jew kidnapped or enslaved a fellow Jew, and no Christian enslaved a believer of the same faith. Enslavement applied only for infidels. At the same time, the duty to redeem a fellow believer from enslavement became a religious duty. A new perception of monotheistic society developed. A society of believers is one that defines the civil status of its freeborn members by their faith. The believer remained part of this society even if kidnapped and enslaved by an infidel. Moreover, since the enemy was infidel, the religious society became responsible for protecting its members from apostasy and would redeem them from enslavement. The religious society in Rabbinic Judaism, early Christianity, and Islam set up common economic measures to free their enslaved members and restore them to their home and status. Society was now becoming defined in religious terms.

By the fifth and sixth centuries ransoming Christians became a duty for bishops.[15] The Byzantine state used this to its advantage by delegating to bishops the responsibility for paying ransoms mentioned in wills of members of their dio-

---

2.xxviii.136–43. P.Cair. Masp. 3:67312. Babylonian Talmud, *Bava-Batra 3b, 8a. Ta'anit 22a*. C. Osiek, "The Ransom of Captives: Evolution of a Tradition," *Harvard Theological Review* 74, no. 4 (1981): 365–386.

14 Corpus papyrorum Judaicarum, ed. Victor A. Tcherikover and Alexander Fuks, 3 vols. (Cambridge, MA: Harvard University Press, 1957–1964), 3:473 (=P. Oxy.1205). Mishnah, Ketubbot 4:9. Tosefta, Horayot 2:5–6. Mishnah, Bava-Metzi'a 2:11–14. P.Lond. 6:1915 and 6:1916 (catalogued in Jews and Christians in Egypt: The Jewish Troubles in Alexandria and the Athanasian Controversy Illustrated by Texts from Greek Papyri in the British Museum, ed. H. Idris Bell and W. E. Crum, Greek Papyri in the British Museum 6. (London: British Museum, 1924).

15 P.Cair. Masp. 3:67312.

cese, and by authorizing the church to sell inalienable lands to ransom captives.[16] So, in 540 twelve thousand Christian inhabitants of Sura were ransomed from the Persians by Candidos the bishop of Sergiopolis.[17] However, gaining the authority to ransom captives was sometimes used by a bishop to increase his own political and economic power. Caesarius, the bishop of Arles (ca. 470–542), used his ransoming of prisoners of war to make them his dependents (Klingshirn, "Caesarius of Arles"). Similar cases of manumission of enslaved persons by the Church to benefit monasteries are attested in the letters of Gregory the Great.[18] This seems at first indicative of a new religious custom of social solidarity. Yet, it shows to a gradual increase in the Church's power over the possession of people.[19] This was used by the state against the authority of private slave owners. The Church received from the state other means to turn enslavement to its advantage.

Asylum: A New Form of Enslavement in the Greek East

Christianizing the Roman Empire started in the fourth century and continued for several centuries. Since the First Council of Nicaea (325), over which the emperor Constantine presided, and throughout this period the laws and social structures of the Empire were adapted to assimilate the Church and its leaders as state officials. Newly founded churches and monasteries received imperial grants, estates, concessions, and authority. They also acquired the right of asylum.

Asylum of fugitives was a practice the Church inherited from ancient pagan temples. The Roman emperor Antoni-

---

16 *Novellae Justiniani*, 120; 131.11.

17 Procopius, *De bello Persico*, bk. 2, ch. 5.

18 Gregory the Great, *Registrum epistularum*, bk. 9, no. 232. MacMaster, "The Transformative Impact," 61.

19 Klingshirn, "Caesarius of Arles." Gregory of Tours, *History of the Franks*, bk. 5, ch. 5 and bk. 10, ch.16.

nus Pius (138–161) ordered with regard to "slaves who take refuge at the shrines of gods or at statues of the emperor [...] that if the cruelty of the owner was found to have been intolerable, such slaves should be compulsorily sold" (*The Institutes of Gaius*, bk. 1, tit. 53). Sheltering runaway slaves, whether Christian or not, though, was repeatedly prohibited by Church councils: a slave who entered a monastery without his owner's consent should be sent back; a slave could not become a monk without his owner's consent.[20] However, by the sixth century Justinian's legislation intervened by increasing the authority of the Church over that of private owners.

Justinian granted the Church permission to receive fugitive slaves and dependent peasants who wished to become monks or clerics, on condition that they had committed no crime, apart from their having fled.[21] If the owner could prove that the slave had harmed him, he had one year to reclaim him in the case of clergymen, or three years in the case of monks. The Church was granted a special status as an autonomous entity that offered a refuge outside the bounds defined by the law. However, the status of the fugitive slave was modified only under asylum. Justinian's asylum law offered the slave the opportunity to join the religious, and this increased the Church's property at the expense of private slaveholders. Although the Church was not legally the owner of the slave, it became his possessor. One form of enslavement (under the original private slaveholder) had been substituted by another (under the monastery). Neither was such a monk a free person. He was subordinated, controlled, and possessed by the abbot. Leaving the monastery required the abbot's permission, and would mean returning to being a slave under his

---

20 Karl Joseph Hefele et al., *Histoire des Conciles d'après les documents originaux*, 11 vols. in 21 (Paris: Letouzey et Ané, 1907–1952), 2/2:779ff. M. Melluso, *La schiavitù nell'età giustinianea: disciplina giuridica e rilevanza sociale* (Besançon: Presses universitaires franc-comtoises, 2000), 257–77.

21 *Novellae Justiniani*, 5.2; 123. Melluso, *La schiavitù nell'età giustinianea*, 201–40.

former owner. Asylum was confined to the boundary of the monastery's property, and the fugitive slave was now part of this property.

In Western Europe too, monasteries and bishops acquired slaves as part of their new role as proprietors (Klingshirn, "Caesarius of Arles"). The monastery of St.-Gallen (in today's Switzerland) exchanged the freedom of a woman it held for five slaves of her husband.[22] This wife was probably ransomed by the monastery and so considered part of its *de facto* possessions. The right of monastic asylum was available also to peasants who fled the fiscal obligations of their own registered land (Latin: *coloni adscripticii*). They became dependents of monasteries who could offer them asylum. In the West free men and women gave themselves, their families, and sometimes their lands, as a donation to monasteries. We find contracts that free individuals made with the abbey of Farfa in central Italy in the eighth century, donating themselves and their service to the monastery, sometimes in return for clothes and shoes.[23]

Monasteries hereby gained possession and power over land and men. This complemented concessions the state granted the Church over its landed property and ensured it had the labour to exploit it. Yet, in view of imperial legislation concerning private slaveholders, we can read these measures also as a way to weaken private powers. They reflect the state's increasing intervention in the relationship between private proprietors and their property, for which the Church became an instrument. By using the Church and changing the definition of slavery the state had created a new concept of the enslaved: not as property, but as possession. Furthermore, confinement to a monastery was a novel way of

---

22 *Chartularium Sangallense*, vol. 1, *700–840*, ed. Peter Erhart (St. Gallen: Ostfildern, 2013), 210. Rio, *Slavery after Rome*, 160.

23 *Il Regesto di Farfa, compilato da Gregorio di Catino*, ed. I. Giorgi and U. Balzani, 5 vols. (Rome: Società romana di storia patria, 1879–1914), 2:81 and 2:119. Rio, *Slavery after Rome*, 60.

punishment that Justinian applied to adulterers.[24] This made private slaveholders dependent on the enslavement of foreigners. In the West, a parallel struggle between public and private authorities developed differently: slavery lost its civil distinction and became entangled with other statuses.

De facto **Enslavement in the Latin West**

Unlike the politically unified Greco-Byzantine Eastern Mediterranean in the fifth to seventh centuries, the Latin West at this time was politically fragmented into separate kingdoms and chiefdoms, each with its distinct legal code, social norms, and economic system. The crystallization of late Roman structures and new Germanic elites and governments was a long process and affected all parts of society. Scholars are divided between a narrative of decline or of continuity in socioeconomic structures and these different perspectives affect the way slavery in these regions is studied. Instead of analyzing the history of slavery as a product of economic conditions and social situations, I intend to consider it as an engine of their transformation.

The precarious economic situation overall, poverty in Western Europe, and the incoming migrants led to increasing trade in humans and their labour. Raids, not warfare, were the more common source of slaves. Enslavement of raided populations was supplemented by selling oneself out of crime and debt as well as the abandonment and sale of one's children. For the poor had no means of survival except the value of theirs and their children's bodies. This suited chiefs, for example in England where strong governmental and legal structures barely existed. The enslavers were not the public authority or its military agents but individual landowners who exploited the enslaved in small-scale rural households and larger estates, both of which needed labour. In most villages

---

24 *Novellae Justiniani*, 134.10. Julia Hillner, *Prison, Punishment and Penance in Late Antiquity* (Cambridge: Cambridge University Press 2015), 315–31.

the links between property and ownership were controlled by a mixture of external owners, prosperous middle-ranking owners, and owner-cultivators (Wickham, *Framing the Early Middle Ages*). They entailed different forms of exploitation, land tenure, and enslavement.

The Latin terms for slavery, *servitus/servitium*, were also used for any form of enslavement and service, while the term for slave, *servus/mancipium*, was used for any form of person with a social obligation of service to a *dominus* (lord/master) (see further in chapter 4). This reflects a new situation where different types of civil statuses became mixed through sharing socioeconomic roles (Rio, *Slavery after Rome*). Unlike the Greek East, the Latin West had no unifying legal system to determine the border between free and slave. This line became blurred and developed into a large array of statuses that limited the movement of free persons and kept them in the service of others on whom they became dependent. Slavery gave way to various statuses of obligation, dependency, and duties, which modern historians tend to refer to as "unfreedom," a vague term which this study avoids. This situation provided a greater versatility than the status of slave and was easily manipulated by landlords. Monasteries in particular benefitted from acts and contracts of self-donation by which free people gave themselves, their families, and sometimes their lands to monasteries out of economic necessity. In fact, self-sale agreements were part of a broader social dynamic of providing services and acquiring duties and obligations in return for a means of living.[25]

In the Lombard laws of the eighth century, comparable to sixth-century Egypt, persons who entered into private service could have found themselves and their children retained in enslavement.[26] If they could, they drafted a contract that

---

25 *Il Regesto di Farfa*, ed. Giorgi and Balzani, 2:81, 2:92, 2:119 and 3:452. Rio, "Self-Sale."

26 *Leges Langobardorum 643–866*, ed. F. Beyerle (Witzenhausen: Deutschrechtliche Institut, 1962): Aistulf 22. Rio, *Slavery after Rome*, 57. P.Cair. Masp. 1:67089 and P.Cair. Masp. 3:67204.

stipulated the terms of their service–enslavement and their particular situation for a specified period. This is the key lesson from early medieval slavery: poverty and the lack of overarching central control of the legal system resulted in various new forms of enslavement: *de facto* slavery. It characterized the diverse economic organization in Western Europe, which was no longer dependent on one's civil status. Rather, ties of obligation became forms of enslavement and were hereditary and legally binding. The precarious economic situation in the fifth to seventh centuries of regions previously part of a single empire led to a spectrum of statuses of legal and social dependency. These reflected the diversity of socioeconomic organization in both East and West, but in different ways with different results. In both the Greek East and Latin West forms of enslavement were pivotal in providing a motor for socioeconomic organization. The advent of Islam in the seventh century employed yet another form of enslavement.

Innovative Islam

Like the formation of the Germanic kingdoms in the fifth century the advent of Islam in the seventh century transformed the geopolitical map. It introduced major innovations in the concept of state, society, and religion. Slavery played a major role. While the debate continues about the scale of the Meccan slave trade in pre-Islamic times, scholars agree on the enslaving activities in the pre-Islamic Hejaz (the populated midwest of Arabia). Raids on neighbouring tribes as well as armed conflict between Arab tribes and their non-Arab enemies were the main causes of enslavement, and reflected high demand: slaves were a major way of gaining high status in pre-Islamic Arab tribes.[27] This situation changed abruptly

---

27 Chase F. Robinson, "Slavery in the Conquest Period," *International Journal of Middle East Studies* 49 (2017): 158–63. H. Gilli-Elewy, "On the Provenance of Slaves in Mecca during the Time of the Prophet Muhammad," *International Journal of Middle East Studies* 49 (2017): 164–68.

with the foundation of the Muslim *umma*, Muhammad's society of believers. All Arab tribes became "submitted" (the meaning of the term "Muslim"), bound by a single "submission" (Arabic: *Islam*), which duly created a political, religious, and national entity. Enslavement or debt slavery of an Arab Muslim by a fellow Muslim was not allowed (Franz, "Slavery in Islam").

This new concept of society that Islam introduced was similar to the Christian idea of a spiritual society of believers. Except, Islam managed to make it real. Islam was not some virtual spiritual society; it managed to actualize the idea of a society of believers through the submission of its members to a common political, religious, and national order. It was national in the sense that all Arabs were forced to become Muslims. This was the aim of the wars of apostasy (Arabic: *Ridda*) in 632–634. Solidarity was enforced by the "Constitution of Medina," Muhammad's founding document which ensured that a member of the *umma* who was captured by the infidel enemy would be ransomed by his tribe, while the ransom money was to be shared by all tribes (see Serjeant, "The Sunnah Jāmi'ah"). The *umma* created a civic notion of a society of believers: its members could not be enslaved and, if captured by an enemy, must be ransomed. The early Caliphate thus succeeded in merging the Roman concepts of State and Church. This had major consequences on slavery: it eliminated the possibility of enslaving Arabs, who became free fellow Muslims. The Muslim ("submitted") Arabs who had owned and traded in slaves for their everyday life and their social status needed to look elsewhere, namely non-Arabs and non-Muslims.

Sources, whether Arabic, Greek, Syriac, Armenian, Coptic, or others that narrate the Arabic Muslim conquests (632–721) and the wars that followed, paint a similar picture: through conquests the newcomers managed to enslave their opponents. This happened to thousands of Cypriots captured in two Muslim attacks in the seventh century.[28] Several trea-

---

28 Attested in an inscription: see Feissel, "Bulletin épigraphique," *Revue des Études Grecques* 100 (1987): 380–81, no. 532.

ties that were signed ensured an annual supply of slaves to the caliph, or forced them to sell their children to pay the new taxes.[29] The conquest of North Africa and Iberia in particular resulted in the enslavement of thousands of captives who were coerced to go east.[30] The conquests were a means of enslavement and not only an objective to gain and hold on to new territories. They also provided the conditions to create a social elite for the Caliphate. Two forms of social dependency reinforced it: the patronage/clientele system (Arabic: *walā'*) by which non-Arabs converted and became the clients of Muslim Arabs, and the enslavement of non-Muslims as the main labour for both private and public bodies (Crone, *Slaves on Horses*).

The religious aspect notwithstanding, it is striking how much these two forms resembled the way Roman society of the early Empire created its elite: using surrendered aliens as freed clients and prisoners of war as slaves. We see this in treaties that the early Caliphate signed with its adversaries in North Africa, the Sahara, or Persia: a special clause determined the number of slaves to be handed annually to the

---

29 al-Balādhurī, *Kitāb Futūḥ al-Buldān*, 193, 279, 292–93, 314–16, 319, 331–33, 457, 553–56, 568–69 (cf. 301–2). Ibn ʿAbd al-Ḥakam, *The History of the Conquest of Egypt, North Africa and Spain: Known as Futūḥ Miṣr wa-akhbāruhā*, ed. Charles C. Torrey (New Haven: Yale University Press, 1922), 188–89 and Ibn ʿAbd al-Ḥakam, *Conquête de l'Afrique du nord et de l'Espagne / Futūḥ Ifrīqiya wa-l-Andalus*, ed. Albert Gateau, 2nd ed. (Algiers: Carbonel, 1948): 34–36. *Ḥudūd al-ʿĀlam. "The Regions of the World": A Persian Geography, 372 A.H. / 982 A.D*, trans. V. Minorsky (London: Oxford University Press, 1970), 112, 345–46, 450. M. Hinds and H. Sakkout, "A Letter from the Governor of Egypt Concerning Egyptian Nubian Relations in 141/758," in *Studia Arabica et Islamica: Festschrift for Iḥsān ʿAbbās on His Sixtieth Birthday*, ed. W. al-Qāḍī (Beirut: American University of Beirut), 209–29. Pipes, *Slave Soldiers and Islam*, 142. Bruning, "Household Slavery in Arabic Documents" (forthcoming) for the Baḳṭ between Nubia and Egypt.

30 Ibn ʿIdhārī, *Kitāb al-bayān al-mughrib*, 1:38, 1:51, 1:141–42. Ibn ʿAbd al-Ḥakam, *Conquête de l'Afrique du nord et de l'Espagne*, ed. Albert, 310–11. Ibn Ḥawḳal, *La configuration de la Terre*, 1: 51–52.

Caliphate. In other words, the Umayyad Caliphate and the later Abbasid Caliphate used means familiar from the Roman Empire and its elite, but introduced innovative methods to use them while employing religious identity as *Realpolitik* in forming the *umma* ("society of Muslims"). They enslaved whoever opposed the new order and taxed everyone else. The taxation system, characteristic of the early Caliphate, established a social and political hierarchy in which the conquered population was subjugated through special taxes (Arabic: *djizya/jizya, ḥaradj/kharaj*) paid to the Arab elite. Those who did not have the means enslaved their children or themselves, or became fugitives in search of a patron (Arabic: *mawlā*) who would convert them to Islam and become their protector/patron/master. Slavery therefore was a way to subjugate non-Muslims through a form of complete control. Its adaptive character and the fact that its definition was an outcome of the interplay between the public and the private, made slavery central to the creation and development of these new medieval civilizations. The following chapters will go on to explore the private and public sides of this phenomenon.

Conclusion

This chapter has traced slavery over a period of great political, economic, and cultural changes which transformed a single Roman Empire into a mosaic of medieval political entities, with distinct cultures, beliefs, languages, laws, and social structures. These changes had crystallized by the eighth century and its results are still with us today. It has determined how the map would look like for more than a millennium to come. From an imperial Roman perspective, a period certainly came to an end: the Empire failed to maintain its political, social, cultural, and religious structures. Whether we call that decline or not depends on our perspective. However, we cannot judge this period as a period of decline in social structures, trade recessions, economic contraction, or waning of religious institutions. Yes, such phenomena occurred, but this was not the entire picture. Its converse was the formation of new governments, new societies, new economies, new religions, and new legal codes.

Chapter 2 challenged the concept of the Roman Empire as a "slave society." If we free ourselves from this term, we must also free ourselves from the idea of "decline." If there was no "slave society" and no "decline," there was no "decline of slavery," an idea which is the result of these two axiomatic theses. Drastic changes certainly occurred in all aspects of public and private life, but slavery did not decline as a result. On the contrary, slavery was active in these processes. Climatic catastrophes, political instability, invasions, conquests, and the waning of imperial legal control had consequences on private and public social organizations. These led to precarious social conditions and poverty, which fuelled the slave trade and led to the enslavement of many, including children. Enslavement, in other words, facilitated a social mobility that was used by both enslaved and enslaver. It provided the former with means to survive under the control of the latter, and the latter with the means to increase domination and power, in both states and tribal societies.

The civil status of a freeborn became dependent on circumstance (*de facto* status), rather than on law (*de jure* status). Slavery did not decline but forms of enslavement changed. This is exemplified in the status of the captive. Enslaved *de facto*, captives retained their legal status in their country of origin thanks to their religious identity as believers whether they were Christians, Muslims, or Jews. The concept of religious identity was used by the Muslim Arabs to create a new type of State: the *umma*. Equivalent to the Latin *civitas*, the *umma* maintained and protected the civil status of its members as submitted ("Muslim") believers.

As for *de jure* slavery, outside Byzantium, neither the Caliphate, nor the other early medieval states had a legal definition of slavery. Naturally they all refer to the ownership and possession of other persons, but left their definition open. This ensured that forms of *de facto* slavery were governed by individual social contexts, not an overarching definition. Slavery became a product of circumstances of *de facto* enslavement. In this it reflected changes in politics, society, and economic poverty. Moreover, we can conclude that the great changes of this era depended on these new forms of enslavement and their legal regulations which provided these newly establish medieval societies with social elasticity. This led to various developments of the Roman institution of slavery, adapted to the particular conditions and needs of each of the Mediterranean societies that grew from the Roman Empire. In the fifth to seventh centuries we can therefore no longer speak of slavery but of slave*ries*. In other words, different circumstances in the east, west, and the south of the Mediterranean required different modes of enslavements. This brought about distinct societies and structures. The following two chapters will analyze the social relations that the new forms of enslavement enabled and the common economic rationale that supported them. These were two complementary aspects of the historical process of slavery in the eighth to tenth centuries.

Chapter 4

New Polities, New Societies, New Economies
Eighth to Tenth Centuries

The previous chapter challenged the theory that the decline of slavery was one of the products of the passage from Antiquity to the Middle Ages. Nevertheless, the Latin terminology of slavery reveals a change in the meaning of the terms "slave," "slavery," or "enslavement" (Latin: *servus* and *servitium/servitus*). By the eleventh and twelfth centuries these terms began to be employed to designate the status of serfs, the medieval dependent peasants in Western and Central Europe, who were legally attached to the land they cultivated. Their obligations and services to the landowner, their "servitude," were designated by the term *servitium/servitus* (Bloch, "Comment et pourquoi finit l'esclavage antique"). This marks the establishment of a new socioeconomic system in Western Europe: serfdom. But what happened between these two periods? What was the meaning of these terms in Western Europe between the eighth and the eleventh centuries? And what were their equivalents in the neighbouring medieval Mediterranean societies? Such questions invite us to reflect on the language of slavery.

The Language of Slavery, Servitude, and Social Dependency

Roman and medieval Latin employ the term *servus* for a male slave, *ancilla* for a female, *mancipium* for both, along with *puer* ("boy") for a young male slave; *libertus* and later *aldius* were employed for freedmen. What is remarkable about the use of these terms in early medieval Latin legal formularies and other documents is the inconsistency in the juridical meaning of these terms. They refer sometimes to slaves, sometimes to freedmen, or to free persons. *Servus* or *mancipium* could designate a person enslaved in the household or for agricultural work in the countryside, a tenant, and even a slaveholder tenant who was under legal obligations to a landowner (Rio, *Slavery after Rome*). Medieval Latin documents use the terms *servus* and *mancipium* to designate states of legal dependency vis-à-vis a slaveholder, a landowner, or any party towards whom these persons had legal obligations. In other words, *servus* came to designate someone who was legally dependent on another party, and his dependency consisted in providing services. In the Carolingian empire cases of self-sale, self-donation, debt bondage, were all translated into a person-to-person relationship in the form of a legal dependency. Such situations blurred the notion of "free status," since whatever civil status such persons had, their legal dependency on another party through land tenure, land possession, or ownership, made them *de facto* "bound" to a separate party in contrast to persons who did not have such ties and obligations.

Such forms of dependency resembled the personal dependency of freedmen towards their former owner, their manumitter, since manumission was a way of creating a legal status of dependency. Moreover, by using the freedman as a gift to a third party for a wide range of different deployments, manumission created social bonds. The great variety of social and economic arrangements set by acts of manumission instituted different forms of personal dependencies to the benefit of the manumitter. Ecclesiastical institutions sometimes acted as a third party in the formation of such legal relationships. In this way the meaning of the term *servus* in Western Europe became much broader than that of being a slave: it covered a spectrum of different legal situations and statuses. In contrast to the narrow Latin vocabulary of slavery, there existed rich local terminologies of states of enslavement whose development reveals the dynamic of slavery. David Pelteret (in *Slavery in Early Mediaeval England*) traced over forty words in Old English that denote states and aspects of slavery and freedom in early medieval Britain. Among the main terms for a slave were *þeow* (from *þeowian*, "to serve"), *witeþeow* (enslaved as punishment) and *þræl/ thrall*, which probably entered English from Old Norse, denoting an enslaved person beholden to a master.

In the East too, the Greek language of the first millennium reveals a large linguistic diversity.[1] The ancient Greek terms for slaves continued to be used in Byzantium. These were *doulos*, *oiketēs*, *therapōn* for a male, *doulē*, *oiketis*, *therapaina/therapainis* for a female, *andrapodon* for both, and *pais/ paidarion* and *paidiskē* (literally "boy" and "girl") for young enslaved. Medieval Greek added to these *oiketikon prosōpon* ("slave figure"), *oiketikon sōma* ("slave body"), *psuharion* ("little soul"), or *katadoulos* for the enslaved, and *sundoulos* for a "co-slave." In addition to the Classical Greek term for freedman and freedwoman (Greek: *apeleutheros*, *apeleuthera*, literally "from free man/woman"), medieval Greek coined the terms *apodoulos/apodoulē* (literally "from slave").

Although *oiketēs/oiketis* originated from the Greek term for household (*oikos*) the terms did not refer exclusively to what scholars call domestic slaves, or slaves of the household. The different terms were largely used as synonyms regardless of what their original meaning was. Moreover, just like in the Latin West they were not used exclusively to designate slaves. The most common terms, *doulos* and *oiketēs*, were employed to refer also to people who were the subordinates of others to whom they owed a service. The Greek term *douleia* designated slavery but also service as well as labour,

---

I Rotman, *Byzantine Slavery and the Mediterranean World*. Günter Prinzing, "Sklaven oder freie Diener im Spiegel der „Prosopographie der mittelbyzantinischen Zeit" (PmbZ)," in *Prosopon Rhomaikon: ergänzende Studien zur Prosopographie der mittelbyzantinischen Zeit*, ed. Alexander Beihammer, Bettina Krönung, and Claudia Ludwig (Berlin: De Gruyter, 2017), 129–73.

and in fact any relation of personal dependency. However, in Greek legal language (both in private and public documents) a strict terminological separation was kept between slaves and non-slaves: *doulos/doulē* and *oiketēs/oiketis* exclusively designated slaves. And here lies the big difference between the Greek East and the Latin West. While Byzantine law provided a clear distinction between the legal status of the enslaved and the enslaver, in the Latin West the legal terminology expressed a change of perspective vis-à-vis slavery: it referred to different legal situations of personal dependency, all designated by the same terms.

Just as in medieval Greek, medieval Arabic terminology for the enslaved is diverse. The common terms are *'abd* or *mamlūk* (literally "owned") for males, *'abd*, *mamlūk*, *rakīk*, *amah*, *djawārī* for women, and *ghulām* and *jāriya* (for "boy" or "youth" and "girl" respectively), as well as *waṣā'if/wuṣafā* (maidservants/pages).[2] As in Byzantium, the literary genre determined the use of the term. Unlike in medieval Greek and Latin, the Arabic terminological diversity developed to reflect the multiplicity in uses of slaves. So, for example, the terms *mamlūk* and *ghulām* came to designate a particular form of military enslavement (see below). *Khādim*, which literally meant "servant," was used in the western regions of the Caliphate to designate castrated slaves, while in the Maghreb it was frequently used to designate a slave of sub-Saharan origin.

Despite similarities, particularly in the language of the slave trade (see chapter 5 below), different developments in the language of slavery in contemporaneous medieval cultures reveal the different developments this institution underwent in each. In all of them the language of slavery was used to denote a social and legal relationship of personal dependency, but they varied by traditions and by type of sources. This shared tendency is seen in terms for God as "the Lord" (Greek: *ho kurios*, Latin: *dominus*, Arabic: *al-Rabb*, Hebrew: *haAdon*), the king, the emperor, or "master." Whether slave-

---

2 R. Brunschvig, "'Abd," in *Encyclopaedia of Islam*, 2nd ed. (Leiden: Brill, 1995–); also available online (paywall).

holder or not, the term "slave" (Greek: *doulos*, Latin: *servus*, Arabic: *'abd*, Hebrew: *'eved*) was used to designate someone who provided a service to the king or the emperor.

Besides these terms, however, other words were used to designate the enslaved. The term "Slavs" (Greek: *sklavoi*, Arabic: *ṣaḵâliba*), was used to designate people trafficked from Eastern Europe by their topo-"ethnic" origin, clear skin, and bright eyes (see Meouak, *Ṣaqâliba*). Other topo-"ethnic" terms were used to designate slaves: for example, "Serbs" (Greek: *serbloi*) came to designate slaves in medieval vernacular Greek from the enslavement of the Serb population and their trafficking into Byzantium.[3] In the same way, the term *Zanj/Zindj* referred to Africans who were trafficked from East Africa and enslaved in large quantities to drain salt marshes and undertake other hard labour in southern Iraq (see al-Ṭabarī, *The Revolt of the Zanj*). This neatly brings us to the question of slave exploitation.

New Patterns of Rural Organization

Although the transatlantic forms of slavery in the antebellum US South, the Caribbean, and Brazil were oriented at rural exploitation through plantations, their economic importance was not necessarily confined to agriculture. On the contrary, recent scholarship connects plantations to the industrial revolution and the rise of modern capitalism (above pp. 34–35). Medieval economies were different. They were predominately agricultural and tightly linked to the form of habitation. However, from Francia to Iraq the medieval world reveals a large diversity in patterns of rural organization which made substantial use of enslavement in various forms.

Scholars tend to ignore the rural exploitation of servile labour in Late Antiquity and the early Middle Ages since the absence of evidence is mostly taken as evidence of absence. But the labour of the enslaved constituted a vital part of the

---

3 Constantine Porphyrogenitus, *De administrando imperio*, ed. Gyula Moravcsik (Washington, DC: Dumbarton Oaks, 1967), ch. 32.

maintenance and expansion of independent economic units. Late Greco-Arabic papyri as well as early Arabic papyri from Palestine and Egypt all attest to the sale of and trade in slaves, most of them of African origin.[4] They reveal households of moderate social status in which the presence of slaves was the norm, and suggest a continuum from Byzantine Egypt to the early Islamic period.[5] It would be wrong to classify this as "domestic slavery," since the household in the early Caliphate, just like in Byzantium and the Latin West, did not refer to domestic space, but designated private social units based on an independent economic setting in both rural and urban milieux.

We are generally poorly informed about the economic organization of the countryside in the Caliphate before the ninth century, especially as far as private landownership is concerned.[6] Nevertheless, we find sporadic mentions of enslaved rural workers, for example during the conquest of southern Iraq and Persia.[7] A unique description, from Anastasius, abbot of St. Catherine's monastery on Mount Sinai in the seventh century, records large numbers of Cypriots, captured and enslaved by Muslims, sowing on public lands.[8] The Zanj, who were trafficked from East Africa by sea are an informative exception. Their three revolts in southern Iraq in 685, 694, and 760 suggest that slavery had a central role in the economy of the early Caliphate.[9] According to the late ninth and early tenth century historian al-Ṭabarī

---

4 Rāġib, *Actes de vente d'esclaves*. Bruning, "Household Slavery in Arabic Documents."

5 Cf. Sassanian Persia and the following note.

6 Hugh Kennedy, "The Feeding of the Five Hundred Thousand: Cities and Agriculture in Early Islamic Mesopotamia," *Iraq* 73 (2011): 177–99.

7 al-Balādhurī, *Kitāb Futūh al-Buldān*, 546–47. Ḥudūd al-ʿĀlam. *"The Regions of the World"*, trans. Minorsky, 127.

8 St. Anastasius Sinaita, *Quaestiones et responsiones*, quaestio 96, in his *Opera omnia*, ed. J.-P. Migne, Patrologia Graeca 89 (Paris: Migne, 1857–1866), 745–46 (available online).

9 Franz, "Slavery in Islam." Savage, "Berbers and Blacks."

the Zanj were exploited in great numbers in draining the salt marshes in southern Iraq as well as in the cultivation of these lands and the transport of rural products. Their owners lived in the towns of southern Iraq and used local managers to control thousands of enslaved Africans who worked on their lands. Their form of enslavement as chattel as well as their special terminological designation and the unique place they hold in Arabic historiography might suggest that theirs was an exceptional case of enslavement which did not comply to Islamic legal norms of slavery. Indeed al-Ṭabarī dedicated a book in his history of the world to their revolts and this has given them historical importance. It was a longlasting phenomenon that affected the history of the Abbasid Caliphate.

In this context the disposability of slave labour, their high price (chapter 5), and the versatile types of slavery make a powerful contrast with plantation slavery of the colonial era. The Zanj joined other mass enslavements in the Abbasid Caliphate involving drainage, cultivation, and building works, for which there was both a steady and predictable supply and demand. These depended mostly on the less expensively priced enslaved Africans. Building mosques, aqueducts, main roads, and palaces required labour on a large scale. Slavery was used alongside wage workers (Franz, "Slavery in Islam"). We have more evidence about enslavement than on the actual enslaved people during the conquests period and the early Caliphate because the historical sources from the early Caliphate were generally not interested in them. However, the sporadic evidence that survives paints a varied picture of economic and social exploitation of the enslaved, which complements and explains the diversity of Arabic vocabulary of slavery.

In Byzantium too, evidence about rural organization before the tenth century is sporadic. A vivid account is given in the *Nomos geōrgikos* (The Farmer's Law), a collection of regulations concerning rural organization from the eighth century. This document reveals ways of protecting the Byzantine farmer's property. It aims at solving disputes between peasants and prescribes punishments for a long list of offences.

The collection paints a clear picture of the Byzantine village being composed of small independent landowning farmers. Slaves (Greek: *douloi*) were used as a rural labour force and are mentioned alongside rural waged workers (*misthioi*, *ergatai*).[10] Although their number is unspecified, we can fill in the picture using archaeology as well as literary descriptions of the Byzantine village and conclude that slaves were employed by Byzantine landowning framers along with waged workers in small quantities due to the small scale and dimensions of landed property.[11]

Apart from small-scale landowning peasants, Byzantine sources pay increasing attention in the ninth and tenth centuries to the rich and powerful elite. These "powerful" people (Greek: *dunatoi*) acquired their wealth mostly through large estates that they held through control of the fiscal obligations of its cultivators.[12] The peasants, whether tenants, land proprietors, or both, became dependents of the powerful through their land obligations. The fiscal obligations of the land they cultivated, possessed, or owned, established a social relationship of personal dependency between them and "the powerful." This peasant dependency was different from the dependency of the enslaved. It was not defined according to a legal distinction like the one between slaves and free persons but was determined by the fiscal status of the land that the

---

10 *Jus Graecoromanum*, ed. Zepos, 2:68–70.

11 Wickham, *Framing the Early Middle Ages* relies on hagiography for describing the structure of the Byzantine village. For Byzantine Italy: G. Noyé, "Quelques observations sur l'évolution de l'habitat en Calabre du Ve au XIe siècle," *Rivista di studi bizantini e slavi* 25 (1988): 57–138 and for central Italy: P. Toubert, *Les structures du Latium médiéval: le Latium méridional et la Sabine du IXe siècle à la fin du XIIe siècle*, 2 vols. (Rome: École française de Rome, 1973).

12 N. Oikonomides, "The Social Structure of the Byzantine Countryside in the First Half of the Xth Century," *Byzantina Symmeikta* 10 (1996): 105–25. Eric McGeer, *The Land Legislation of the Macedonian Emperors* (Toronto: Pontifical Institute of Mediaeval Studies, 2000).

farmer cultivated.[13] Yet slaves, especially manumitted slaves, were far from rare in rural society in Asia Minor. In fact, it was the only way for independent peasants to enrich their estates and improve their economic status when facing the growing influence of the rich magnates who imposed their rural taxes. A Byzantine tax treaty of the tenth century describes the land organization of small-scale landowning peasants and the ways in which they could improve the small farms on which they live by employing livestock and slaves.[14]

Slavery was thus used as both a tool for cultivation and wealth creation. However, slaves were an expensive labour force. Exploiting the peasantry, the Byzantine imperial elite developed a new form of social dependency from which it could profit much more easily than through slavery. Direct use of slavery was no longer necessary to attain a position of power. However, the enslaved continued to be used as a labour force by the peasantry. In fact, it was the only way for small-scale farmers to survive the new form of dependency afflicted on them by the state and the elite who acted as its agents.

In Byzantium, the Latin West, and the Caliphate, large estates with large quantities of slaves were not unusual. One example is Philaretos, an eighth-century saint, whose *Life* was written a century later.[15] This source depicts the life of an eighth- to ninth-century magnate in the Black Sea coast of northcentral Anatolia who owned large estates, livestock, and many slaves. His plunge into a life as a poor farmer was marked by the loss of his estates and slaves. He was left with the field around his house and a couple of slaves to cultivate it. Another example is Eustathios Boïlas, a magnate from east-

---

13 Youval Rotman, "Formes de la non-liberté dans la campagne byzantine aux VIIe–XIe siècles," *Mélanges de l'École Française de Rome, Moyen Âge* 112, no. 2 (2000): 499–510.

14 Franz Dölger, *Beiträge zur Geschichte der byzantinischen Finanzverwaltung besonders des 10. und 11. Jahrhunderts* (Hildesheim: Teubner, 1964): 113–56.

15 *The Life of St. Philaretos the Merciful Written by His Grandson Niketas*, ed. L. Rydén (Uppsala: Studia Byzantina Upsaliensia, 2002).

ern Asia Minor, whose will refers to his large estate and various properties which he leaves to his daughters along with the slaves (Greek: *psukharia*).[16] In contrast to those slaves left to his daughters, Boïlas manumits some of his slaves (*oiketai*) and bequeaths them modest parcels of land.

Unlike Byzantium and the Caliphate, in Western Europe the meaning of the term slave/*servus* itself was determined by social conditions and not by a legal distinction between slaves and free persons. In fact, social status determined the legal status of the peasant. Carolingian legal documents reveal no systematic distinction between unfree labour and tenancy, and no clear difference between tenants of free and unfree status (Rio, *Slavery after Rome*). The obligations of service and duties of the farmer were determined by the status of his land, quite distinct from the farmer's personal status. So, the farmer's status depended on the land's status and this became more important than the farmer's *de jure* status. Polyptychs, documents describing tenant holdings by estate of major Carolingian monasteries show special status being assigned to estates through the labour duties that the land acquired. These duties of the land, imposed on the farmer, made his legal status as free or slave unclear and dependent more and more on the status of the land on the one hand, and on the obligation, or "service," that it imposed. This made the freeborn (Latin: *ingenui*) appear like slaves, while slaves who worked on the same manses could appear like the free.[17] People offered themselves and their families to monasteries and

---

16 Lemerle, *Cinq études*, 15–63. Paul Magdalino, "The Byzantine Aristocratic *oikos*," in *The Byzantine Aristocracy IX–XIII Centuries*, ed. M. Angold (Oxford: British Archaeological Reports, 1984), 92–111.

17 *Das Polyptychon von Saint-Germain-des-Prés. Studienausgabe*, ed. D. Hägermann, K. Elmshäuser, and A. Hedwig (Cologne: Böhlau, 1993). *Le Polyptyque et les listes de cens de l'abbaye de Saint-Remi de Reims*, ed. Jean-Pierre Devroey (Reims: Académie nationale, 1984). Rio, *Slavery after Rome*, 177–212. J. Barbier, "'The Praetor Does Concern Himself with Trifles.' Hincmar, the Polyptych of St-Rémi and the Slaves of Courtisols," in *Auctoritas: mélanges offerts*

private landowners for life, or part of their life, or part of the week, in return for land, food and clothing, or in return for the removal of debts. Some kept their status as free persons, others did not. In fact, since the status of tenant was determined *de facto* through the status of the land and the obligations it imposed, there was no need to define it *de jure*. In contrast to both Byzantium and the Caliphate, in Carolingian Francia the legal definition that set a clear distinction between slave and free person became irrelevant for the organization of rural society.[18] Its ambiguity proved more beneficial to landowners who could more easily enslave persons through the services and obligations of the land on which they worked.

In medieval Europe other societies also made extensive use of slavery, societies which are less well documented, such as early medieval England, Scandinavia, and east-central Europe. These were societies with no strong central authority, were still largely tribal, and where raids and enslavement of captives played a major role. Raiding was a means to enlarge the population of the tribe or chiefdom. Viking Iceland for example was populated by enslaved Irish. They enriched the enslavers who became also slave traders.[19] There too, *servi* or *mancipia* are documented on rural estates. This was the situation in Bavaria and Hungary, and is also attested in the eleventh century for England and Wales in the Domesday Book.[20] The enslaved were a merchandise

---

à Olivier Guillot, ed. Giles Constable and Michel Rouche (Paris: Presses de l'Université de Paris–Sorbonne, 2006), 267–79.

18 But still important: *Le Polyptyque et les listes de cens […] de Reims*, 26–30.

19 Karras, *Slavery and Society in Medieval Scandinavia*. S. Sunna Ebeneserdóttir et al. (2018) "Ancient Genomes from Iceland Reveal the Making of a Human Population," *Science* 360, no. 6392 (2018): 1028–32.

20 Carl Hammer, *A Large-Scale Slave Society of the Early Middle Ages: Slaves and Their Families in Early Medieval Bavaria* (Aldershot: Ashgate, 2002). Cameron Sutt, *Slavery in Árpád-era Hungary in a Comparative Context: East Central and Eastern Europe in the Middle Ages, 450–1450* (Leiden: Brill, 2015). Pelteret, *Slavery in Early Mediaeval England*.

too in demand by the richer Mediterranean societies for various economic roles.

The Craft, Business, and Urban Economy

Some estates in Western Europe included textile workshops where enslaved women worked. The forms of exploitation and control over enslaved women had other specific aspects to which we will return below. Slaves constituted a part of the private household. Scholars tend to call this "domestic slavery." But medieval households were complex socioeconomic organizations far from based on domestic labour. A unique source from tenth-century Constantinople clarifies the economic functions of slaves in urban households.

The *Book of the Prefect* of Constantinople is a collection of regulations according to which the Prefect or Eparch of Constantinople controlled the city's economic organization. It offers a unique evidence of the place of slaves in the urban economy of Byzantium as official members in the different guilds, whether as managers, shopkeepers, or foremen.[21] Slaveholders could set their slaves as notaries, silversmiths, goldsmiths, ironsmiths, moneychangers, laundresses, candle makers, soap makers, grocers, saddlers, butchers, cattle and pig merchants, fishmongers, bakers, innkeepers, carpenters, masons, painters, and silk manufacturers. Opening a business required acceptance by the guild of the city corporation, a location, and a workforce, so was a substantial financial investment. Slaves were accepted as members of guilds and business managers. In the Caliphate too, slaves were used in private businesses as shopkeepers, managers of stores, porters, and boatmen.[22]

---

21 *Das Eparchenbuch Leons des Weisen*, ed. Johannes Koder (Vienna: Österreichischen Akademie der Wissenschaften, 1991), chs. 3.1, 4.2, 6.7, 7.5, 8.7, and 8.13.

22 Ibn Muḥammad Baihaḳī, *al-Mahāsin wa'l-Masāwi'*, ed. F. Schwally (Leipzig: Giessen, 1902), 613–15. Savage, "Berbers and Blacks." Franz, "Slavery in Islam."

A Byzantine businessman could start a business more easily using his slaves, since this required a single guarantor, himself, in contrast to five guarantors in case of a free person.[23] All profits went to the owner, and in case of fines, the slave was confiscated, while no fine was imposed on the owner.[24] Businessmen relied heavily on acquiring slaves whom they could train in particular professions and then set them up as their managers and workers. Wage labour was much less attractive than enslaved labour. Employment of wage workers was limited by contracts of one month maximum and wages needed to be paid in advance; no such restrictions applied of course in the case of slaves. Analysis of these regulations reveals that the urban economic system was organized in private households and depended on their ability to employ enslaved labourers with no legal entity that could make them liable. In other words, the organization and success of urban enterprises depended on slavery. A rich household that held five to ten slaves or more could manage several business organizations for which slaves were used as economic agents. And yet, acquiring humans as agents was an expensive business.

Cost of Slave Labour

Human merchandise was extremely expensive in Mediterranean medieval societies. This was mainly due to the long journeys and difficult means employed in procuring the enslaved (see further in chapter 5). Prices of European male slaves varied between twenty gold coins in Constantinople and thirty gold dinars and more in Egypt.

---

23 *Das Eparchenbuch Leons des Weisen*, ch. 2.9.

24 *Das Eparchenbuch Leons des Weisen*, ch. 12.9.

Date	Place	Details	Price	Source
9th cent.	Constantinople	tax on one enslaved person	2 nom.	Theophanes Confessor, Chronographia, ed. C. De Boor, 2 vols. (orig. 1883–1885; repr. Hildesheim: Olms, 1963), 1:487
9th cent.	Constantinople	enslaved person	10 nom.	Jus Graecoromanum, ed. Zepos, 2:153
11th cent.	Constantinople	price of an enslaved person	20 nom.	Jus Graecoromanum, ed. Zepos, 4:83–84
1050	Asia Minor	price of an enslaved murderer, sold to a bishop	24 nom.	G. A. Rhallēs and M. Potlēs, eds., Syntagma tōn theiōn kai hierōn kanonōn tōn te hagiōn kai paneuphēmōn Apostolōn, 6 vols. (Athens: Grigoris, 1966), 5:48–49
9th cent.	Egypt	enslaved woman	10–30 dinar	Rāġib, Actes de vente d'esclaves
10th cent	Egypt	enslaved woman	13–25 dinar	Rāġib, Actes de vente d'esclaves
10th to 12th cent.	Egypt	average price of an enslaved woman	20 dinar	Goitein, A Mediterranean Society, 1:136–40, 1:434n64 and Goitein, "Slaves and Slave Girls in the Cairo Geniza Records," Arabica 9, no. 1 (1962): 1–20
995	Egypt	enslaved Byzantine (Rumiyya) woman	Estimated at 80 dinar	Goitein, A Mediterranean Society, 1:137–38, 1:433n45
11th cent.	Egypt	enslaved woman	15–40 dinar	Goitein, A Mediterranean Society, 1:137–39, 1:433–34nn38–40, 64; T.-S. 13 in Mann (1969): 2:88
969	Syria	value of a man/woman/child refugee	30/20/15 dinar	Ibn al-ʿAdīm, Zubdat, ed. Zakkar, 1:155

Table 1: Prices of Slaves in the Eastern Mediterranean, 800– 1100[25] (nom. = nomisma, Byzantine gold coin).[26] *[Left]*

If we want to know how expensive enslaved persons in the Middle Ages were in comparative terms, we need to compare their price to other goods and analyze the purchasing power in medieval markets, as indicated in the table overleaf.

---

25 Rāǧib, *Actes de vente d'esclaves*. Eliyahu Ashtor, *Histoire des prix et des salaires dans l'Orient médiéval* (Paris: S.E.V.P.E.N., 1969). Jean-Claude Cheynet, E. Malamut, and Cécile Morrison, "Prix et salaires à Byzance (Vᵉ-XVᵉ siècles)," in *Hommes et richesses dans l'Empire byzantin*, vol. 2, *VIIIᵉ–XVᵉ siècle*, ed. V. Kravari, J. Lefort, and C. Morrison (Paris: Lethielleux, 1991), 339–74. Cécile Morrison and Jean-Claude Cheynet, "Prices and Wages in the Byzantine World," in *The Economic History of Byzantium*, ed. Angeliki Laiou, 3 vols. (Washington, DC: Dumbarton Oaks, 2002), 2:815–78).

26 E. Schilbach, *Byzantinische Metrologie* (Munich: Beck, 1970), 169*ff.* and 185*ff.* Cheynet, Malamut, and Morrison, "Prix et salaires à Byzance." Cécile Morrison, "Byzantine Money: Its Production and Circulation," in *The Economic History of Byzantium*, ed. Angeliki Laiou, 3 vols. (Washington, DC: Dumbarton Oaks, 2002), 3:909–96. Goitein, *A Mediterranean Society*, 1:359–392. McCormick, *Origins of the European Economy*, 344*ff.* Andrew S. Ehrenkreutz, "Studies in the Monetary History of the Near East in the Middle Ages, II: The Standard of Fineness of Western and Eastern Dînârs before the Crusades," *Journal of the Economic and Social History of the Orient* vol. 6, no. 3 (1964): 243–77. W. C. Schultz, "The Monetary History of Egypt, 642–1517," in *The Cambridge History of Egypt*, vol. 1, *Islamic Egypt, 642–1517*, ed. Carl F. Petry (Cambridge: Cambridge University Press, 1988), 318–38. Jacob Mann, *The Jews in Egypt and in Palestine under the Fâtimid Caliphs: A Contribution to their Political and Communal History Based Chiefly on Genizah Material Hitherto Unpublished*, 2 vols. (Oxford: Oxford University Press, 1969).

Table 2: Comparative Prices of Slaves in the Eastern Mediterranean, 800–1100[27]

Comparable Goods or Wage Costs	Male slave in Byzantium (price: 20-25 nomisma)	Male slave in Egypt (price: 33 dinar)	Female slave in Egypt (price: 15-25 dinar)
Livestock	1.5-2 horses	2-3 horses	1.5-2 horses
Land	0.25-1 house in Taranto	3-6 small country houses	1.5-2 small country houses
	2-4 shops in Constantinople	rent for shop for 22 years	rent for shop for 6.6-10 years
Wheat (regular price)	3072-3840 kg (=240-300 *modioi thalasioi*)	3614 kg (=297 *waibat*)	1642-2738 kg (=135-225 *waibat*)
Wages of:			
day labourer	20-100 months	5.5-41 months	2.5-31.25 months
civil servant	5-8 months	4.7-6 months	2-3.5 months
high dignitary	1/3 month	0.18-2 months	0.083-0.36 months

The price of a slave was therefore equivalent to the price of a house in the Byzantine countryside, or three typical shops in Constantinople, a half-year's wage for a Byzantine civil servant and six years of pay for a day labourer. He was worth more than three tonnes of wheat in Byzantium.

Prices of the enslaved were therefore extremely high when seen in relation to the purchasing power in Byzantium. Our long timeframe notwithstanding, these prices remained relatively stable in medieval Mediterranean markets. In the Islamic world too, humans were a highly expensive merchandise. In Fatimid Egypt (an independent Shiite Caliphate that ruled in North Africa and Palestine in the tenth and eleventh centuries) European slaves cost fifty percent more than in Byzantium. Yet, the purchasing power there was double. The price of one slave was equivalent to 3,600 kg of wheat and could pay more than ten years of rent for a shop or a small house in the countryside. It was the equivalent of several

---

27 Rāġib, *Actes de vente d'esclaves*. Ashtor, *Histoire des prix et des salaires*. Cheynet, Malamut, and Morrison, "Prix et salaires à Byzance."

months' salary of a civil servant in Egypt, or three years of a day labourer (half the comparable cost of Byzantium). All this means that slaves were not abundant, they were expensive, and could be purchased only by people of means.

The fact that the price of slaves was a substantial investment made their employment in private medieval households dependent on wealth. Such households could not rely for their expansion on cheap waged workers because, unlike with slaves, they were no engine for the growth of private enterprises. The fact that economic growth was dependent on the enslavement, acquisition, and ownership of people rather than hired labour is clear in the particular economic functions that enslaved women and men filled in medieval societies.

Slavery versus Marriage

The 2017 ILO and Walk Free Foundation report on the state of modern slavery includes forced marriage as a widespread form of enslavement. Forced marriage has had a long and painful history and has constituted an inseparable part of human development. The lifelong subjugation of girls and women by men whom they did not choose has played a fundamental role in many societies. And yet, although forced marriage is a form of enslavement and has destined millions of girls and women to a life of servitude, it is considered distinct from slavery. In fact, the reality for a free-born girl who finds herself trapped in enslaving marriage could be equal or much worse than that of a female slave. Nevertheless, it does not help us to understand the specifics of slavery as a historical process. For that we need to consider what slavery provided that marriage could not, or to put it differently: what is specific about the enslavement of women? There are significant differences in the ways women are enslaved through slavery and through marriage.

First, women could also be enslaved by women. In the Middle Ages such women performed mainly manual work as part of the retinue of aristocratic women, or held roles particular to women, such as wet nurses.[28] It was the possession of enslaved women by male enslavers that gave the second complete control over the body of the former and resulted in many cases in rape, violence, and sexual abuse. It could develop into forced marriage. This form of abuse of women is clarified if we consider marriage not as an institution that joins a man and a woman, but as a contract that joins into a personal relationship between two men: father and husband. With this aim the woman/daughter serves as a sexual and procreative instrument that ensures, in addition, the transmission of property from the maternal grandfather to the son. In other words, the married woman/daughter is the social vector to connect two men, her father and her husband, in order to provide a third male who will be the progeny and heir of both. So, the circumstances of the married woman will depend on the terms under which she is transferred from her father's authority to her husband's. The legal and economic terms regarding property, the legal and economic constraints on breaking the marriage, as well as cultural norms, personal character, and other individual factors determine the level of servitude or freedom of the woman within the marriage. These terms can give the husband full domination over the wife and destine her to enslavement. Equally, they can also limit the power of the husband over the wife.

A female slave, on the other hand, is not a vector connecting anyone. Her status as a slave, in contrast to that of a married woman, ensures that no preliminary conditions or constraining terms limited her exploitation and abuse. It makes the sexual and procreative relationship between a man and a woman solely dependent on the former without any consideration of the woman's family. In other words, it frees the first from any attachment to another man. In other words: a man

---

28 *Six inédits d'hagiologie byzantine*, ed. F. Halkin (Brussels: Société des Bollandistes, 1987), 179–95. See also *Acta Sanctorum: Novembris*, ed. C. De Smedt et al. (repr. 1971; Brussels: Société des Bollandistes, 1910), 3:790–813. *Vie de Sainte Mélanie. Actes d'Iviron*, 2:§47. Ibn Buṭlān. "Risālā," 352. Franz, "Slavery in Islam," 93.

can do whatever he wants with a female slave and he has no legal constraints or social attachment to other men that may limit his power over her. However, in this also lies a disadvantage in such a relationship. If we consider marriage to be an institution to connect men, a means to create family ties, and social, economic, and political relationships, the ownership of female slaves provides none of these benefits. The enslavement of women by men within marriage and the enslavement of women by men within the framework of the institution of slavery follow two distinct rationales. The first provides a way of establishing relationships with other men, while the second is built on the premise that the woman is not related to any other man. Each provides different advantages and disadvantages to the enslaver. The famous rape of the Sabine women by the Romans exemplified this very well (Livy, *The History of Rome*, bk. 1, ch. 9). The rape and abduction of other men's women is an act of war between men, while the unions of men and women with the consent of the women's male relatives create unions between males. In both cases, women are the means to construct social relations between men.[29]

While the institution of marriage can set limits to the domination and objectification of the married woman, ownership of a female slave provides her male enslaver with complete authority to exploit her without any constraints. He can exploit her sexually, make her his concubine, manumit her, and also marry her. The power over her body lies solely in the hand of the male enslaver. Furthermore, Roman legal reforms of the fourth century ensured that this type of domination cannot occur between a female enslaver and an enslaved male.[30]

---

29 Cf. Kecia Ali, *Marriage and Slavery in Early Islam* (Cambridge, MA: Harvard University Press, 2010) for a different view on the Muslim world.

30 *Codex Theodosianus* 9.9.1. Judith Evans Grubbs, "'Marriage More Shameful than Adultery': Slave–Mistress Relationships, 'Mixed Marriages,' and Late Roman Law," *Phoenix* 47 (1993): 125–54 and Evans Grubbs, *Law and Family in Late Antiquity: the Emperor*

Both the medieval Latin West and Greek East inherited the Roman legal definition of marriage as monogamy (Greek *mono-gamos*: literally "single marriage") between a free man and a free woman. Christianity introduced two further significant innovations. The first was a prohibition on divorce: marriage became indissoluble. The second was a prohibition on sexual relations outside marriage. This was aimed, among others, against sexual relationships between an enslaver and the enslaved. The prohibition on enslavers to prostitute their enslaved women dates back to the fifth century, and was elaborated by three emperors (Theodosius II, Leon I, and Justinian).[31] A slave treated in this way who appeared before a magistrate or bishop was freed. A later Byzantine canon forced the enslaver to marry his prostituted enslaved woman on pain of excommunication.[32] A third prohibition was the Christian ban on clergy marrying and having sexual intercourse. Such measures did not always have the desired results. The rich, including churchmen, continued to have illicit unions with their female slaves.[33] In fact, enslavement of women ensured that clergymen could exploit, abuse, and rape women without having to marry them.

In Carolingian Francia marital unions of people of mixed status became instrumental in enabling private lords to perpetuate the ties of dependency onto following generations (Rio, *Slavery after Rome*). In Byzantium, by contrast, the legal Roman definition prevailed: children of any mixed union

---

Constantine's Marriage Legislation (Oxford: Clarendon Press, 1995), 273–77.

31 *Codex Theodosianus* 15.8.2. *Codex Justinianus*, C.11.41.6–7. Buckland, *The Roman Law of Slavery*, 603.

32 J.-B. Pitra, *Juris ecclesiastici Graecorum historia et monumenta*, 2 vols. (Rome: Typis collegii Urbani, 1864–1868), 2:344, canon 182. V. Grumel et al., *Les Regestes des Actes du Patriarcat de Constantinople*, 7 vols. (Paris. Institut français d'Études byzantines, 1932–1979), 1:52–53 §§407–407a.

33 Susan Mosher Stuard, "Ancillary Evidence for the Decline of Medieval Slavery," *Past and Present* 149 (1995): 3–28.

between a free man and a slave woman were slaves. By the ninth century marriage between persons of mixed status became legal.[34] For enslaved couples, Christian marriage became possible. In fact, Byzantine legislation excommunicated enslaved couples who were joined outside the Church.[35] In the eleventh century the Byzantine legislator prohibited any unions between slaves outside Christian marriage.[36] Naturally, slaveholders were reluctant to allow Christian marriage for unions between their slaves, unions that they could not thereafter break and imposed other restrictions in the case of manumission of one of the couple. Opportunities for marriage between slaves went therefore hand in hand with the development of marriage as a Christian institution. In fact, slavery was central to the development of Christian marriage and the change of power relations. In Muslim societies things were different.

Private Subjects, Family, and the Army in Muslim Societies

Monogamy did not apply to Muslim societies. Male polygamy was especially practised by men who had the means to acquire and possess women. It set particular social norms over family structures, while no moral constraints limited the sexual exploitation that enslaver men could have over enslaved women. This encouraged the enslavement of women as either wives or slaves (Ali 2010). The fact that in Sunni law sons inherited the status of their father, regardless of the legal status of their mother, made the enslavement of

---

34 *Les Novelles de Léon le Sage*, ed. P. Noailles and A. Dain (Paris: Belles Lettres, 1944), §§100–101. "Die Novellen des Kaiserin Eirene," ed. L. Burgmann, in *Fontes minores, IV*, ed. Brugmann (Frankfurt: Klostermann, 1981), 1–33 at 26.

35 Pitra, *Juris ecclesiastici Graecorum historia et monumenta*, 2:346, canon 199.

36 *Jus Graecoromanum*, ed. Zepos, 1:401–7.

women a way to expand the family.[37] Such enslaved mothers acquired a new legal status by virtue of being "mother of the children" (Arabic: *um al-walad*) and this prohibited her sale. This turned her into a concubine, and ensured that the enlarged family stayed together (Gordon, "Unhappy Offspring?"). In fact, it was prohibited to sell an enslaved woman without her children. Numerous papyri contracts of sale specify the sale of mothers with their daughters, even granddaughters.[38] Slavery thus ensured much harsher male control over a woman who had no legal social ties, and Muslim jurisprudence ensured that no equivalent attitude existed between a woman and her male slaves (Ali 2010). If we add to that the Muslim prohibition on adoption, we can conclude that polygamy and the enslavement of women in medieval Muslim societies were the main tool for men to expand their lineage, kinship, and power. Enslaved men and boys served as a means for the same objective.

An exceptional form of enslavement developed in early Islam: military slavery.[39] Military slavery refers to a system of acquisition, training, and employing slaves as soldiers. A "military slave" was a person whose enslavement led to a life of military service. This is not some long-gone phenomenon. It can be detected today in African and Asian societies where boys are abducted (or "recruited") by local militias

---

37 Gordon, *Slavery in the Arab World*. Brunschvig, "'Abd," in *Encyclopaedia of Islam*.

38 Rāġib, *Actes de vente d'esclaves*, §§4; 10–11.

39 Berger, "Mamluks in Abbasid Society." E. de la Vaissière, *Samarcande et Samarra. Élites d'Asie centrale dans l'Empire Abbaside* (Paris: Association pour l'Avancement des Études Iranéennes, 2007). Sato Kentaro, "Slave Elites and the Saqāliba in al-Andalus in the Umayyad Period," in *Slave Elites in the Middle East and Africa: A Comparative Study*, ed. Miura Toru and John E. Philips (London: Kegan Paul, 2000), 25–40 and this collection more generally. Bacharach, "African Military Slaves." Crone, *Slaves on Horses*, 49–81. Pipes, *Slave Soldiers and Islam*. Ayalon, *Islam and the Abode of War*. Gordon, *The Breaking of a Thousand Swords*.

(Bogner & Rosenthal, *Child Soldiers in Context*). Unlike the Roman Empire where acquisition and use of slaves as soldiers was unthinkable, this form of enslavement became frequent under the Caliphate. Units of client soldiers of non-Arab origin, converted to Islam through ties of clientage (Arabic: *walā'/mawālī*), were incorporated into the Umayyad army and replaced its traditional tribal-based military structures. In the eighth century the Abbasid caliphs began to introduce foreigners in a systematic manner into their army and integrated their clients as soldiers, practically forming a private army.

The enslavement of Turks as soldiers dates to the early ninth century. They were used as private guards of the brother-caliphs al-Ma'mūn (813–833) and al-Mu'tasim (833–842) to counterbalance the powerful Arab regiments.[40] al-Mu'tasim's foundation of the city of Samarra (about 120 km northwest of Baghdad) with its caliphal guards established a new type of capital for the Caliphate (836–892).[41] The objective was to separate the caliph from the powerful military elites. The caliphal guards and regiments were composed of cliented Turks (*mawālī*) together with enslaved Turks who were trafficked for this purpose from the Steppes and Transoxania.[42] A system of patronage connected the Turkish guards to the caliph on the one hand, and established ties of dependency between themselves and other royal servants on the other hand. The result was a social network that allowed these units to acquire independent power and wealth (Gordon, *The Breaking of a Thousand Swords*). Between 861 and 866, this elite guard revolted against caliph al-Mutawakkil (847–861) and controlled the city of Samarra during a period known as "the anarchy at Samarra" (al-Ṭabarī, *The Crisis of the 'Abbāsid Caliphate*).

---

40 Gordon, *The Breaking of a Thousand Swords*. Berger, "Mamluks in Abbasid Society."

41 al-Ṭabarī, *The Crisis of the 'Abbāsid Caliphate*. De la Vaissière, *Samarcande et Samarra*.

42 De la Vaissière, *Samarcande et Samarra*. Ayalon, *Islam and the Abode of War*. Berger, "Mamluks in Abbasid Society."

The trafficking of enslaved foreigners perpetuated the supply of soldiers to the caliph's dependent regiments. This was the origin of the *mamlūk* institution which formed loyal military elites (see Ayalon, *Islam and the Abode of War*). The enslaved soldiers were personally dependent on their "owner" and removed from all other social groups. The Mamluks (literally "the owned") were imported as boys and trained as the caliph's military elite. The model was copied by local Muslim leaders who needed their own loyal regiments. Although enslaved soldiers were usually manumitted, they retained their status as *mamlūk*. They were converted, could marry, and set up families. We can think of the Mamluks as a client army whose continuation was dependent on enslaved foreigners. These were mainly trafficked from Eurasia, traditionally from the northeast (the Steppes, and Transoxiana), but also from Nubia and Sudan, especially for the emirate armies of North Africa and the Red Sea.[43] In the Maghreb and Fatimid Egypt military slaves of sub-Saharan origin were designated as "youths" (Arabic: *ghilmāns*, or *zawāwila*).[44] Aḥmad ibn Ṭūlūn is an excellent example of the way the system of Mamluks functioned. He was the son of Ṭūlūn, an enslaved Turk who was trafficked to Iraq as part of the tribute of the Samanid governor of Bukhara and served in the private guard of the Caliph al-Ma'mūn in Samarra. Aḥmad ibn Ṭūlūn rose prominently in the caliph's guard and was sent to Egypt in 868 to accompany the Turkish general Bākbāk. When the governor of Palestine revolted Ibn Ṭūlūn organized an independent army of enslaved Turks and Nuba that he later used to form his own independent dynasty as an emir in Egypt and Syria: the Ṭūlūnids.[45]

---

43 Bacharach, "African Military Slaves." Timothy Power, *The Red Sea from Byzantium to the Caliphate: AD 500–1000* (Cairo: The American University in Cairo Press, 2012).

44 Ibn 'Idhārī, *Kitāb al-bayān al-mughrib*, 1:122, 1:133. Trabelsi, "Commerce et esclavage dans le Maghreb oriental." Bacharach, "African Military Slaves." Savage, "Berbers and Blacks."

45 Al-Balawī, *Sīrat Aḥmad ibn Ṭūlūn*, ed. Muḥammad Kurd 'Alī (Cairo: Maktabat al-Thaqāfa al-Dīniyya, 1939). Matthew S. Gordon,

Although the scope to use enslaved soldiers in medieval Islamic armies and its classification as slavery is debated, this phenomenon as well as the rural enslavement of the *Zanj/Zindj* are good examples of the new elastic definition of slavery, which fitted the different needs of these medieval societies as they took form. This was also the case with the trafficking of enslaved castrated boys for the Abbasid, Byzantine, and Andalusian palaces where they formed the imperial elites in the administration and management of the political authority.[46] Like the Mamluks, eunuchs were dependent on trafficking of enslaved foreigners.[47] In al-Andalus, Umayyad Iberia, in particular, the castrated *ṣaḳāliba/ṣaqāliba* ("Slavs"/ slaves) were a sign of the strength and wealth of the political power, capable of surrounding itself with an exclusive administrative elite (Meouak, *Ṣaqāliba*).

Military enslavement and enslavement with castration of men were both key elements of the ruling elites in most medieval Muslim dynasties. Slavery allowed the caliphs to institutionalize exclusive military and court powers from their private subjects, in other words to produce and establish non-biological lineages to support caliphal power. The foundation of the Abbasid Caliphate in the eighth and ninth centuries and the Umayyad Caliphate in al-Andalus in the tenth century both made extensive use of different forms of enslavement. The key factor was the range of possibilities that slavery offered for economic expansion by rendering the

---

"Aḥmad ibn Ṭūlūn and the Politics of Deference," in *Islamic Cultures, Islamic Contexts: Essays in Honor of Professor Patricia Crone*, ed. Asad Q. Ahmed, Behnam Sadeghi, Roger G. Hoyland, and Adam Silverstein (Leiden: Brill, 2014), 226–56. Z. M. Hassan (2012) "Aḥmad b. Ṭūlūn," in *Encyclopaedia of Islam*, 2nd ed. (Leiden: Brill, 1995–); also available online (paywall).

46 Meouak, *Ṣaqâliba*. David Ayalon, *Eunuchs, Caliphs and Sultans: A Study in Power Relationships* (Jerusalem: Magnes, 1999). Shaun Tougher, *The Eunuch in Byzantine History and Society* (London: Routledge, 2008). Kentaro, "Slave Elites and the Saqāliba."

47 Meouak, *Ṣaqâliba*. Procopius, *De bello Gothico*, bk. 4, ch.3.

enslaved as private subjects. This manifested the social isolation of the caliphal power, immersed in a network of relationships it established through enslavement.

The enslavement of foreigners and adversaries and their integration as newly-converted enslaved Muslims was an outcome of the early Muslim conquests. But we can also change perspective and consider the foundation of a new type of religious state with a new elite as being reliant on the subjugation of the non-Arabic population through varying types of personal dependency. Enslavement was key, and conquests, subjugation, trafficking, and trading human beings were the way to achieve it.

So, slavery acquired a new role for those who wished to accumulate political power and was essential for the social development that Islam introduced. It was similar in other Mediterranean societies. Although the Byzantine army, like the armies in the Latin West, was not at all oriented towards employing enslaved soldiers, slaves were part of private militias.[48] In Byzantium too, slaves along with freedmen formed the economic backbone of the private household. Byzantine wills of dignitaries reveal clearly that their status depended on both economic and social wealth. The first meant land assets, the second meant human assets which Byzantine Greek termed "my people" (Greek: *hoi anthrōpoi mou*).[49] Slavery was the means to acquire one's "own people," and manumission was the means to render them private subjects of their enslavers.

In the caliphates these means helped ensure the independence of the leader's political power. In a word, enslavement and manumission together formed a social institution for the creation of private subjects who were required for different aspects of power organization in medieval societies. We shall see in the next chapter that religion influenced this dynamic by providing means for the social integration of the enslaved. This leads us to investigate the ways in which slavery linked two central phenomena: migration and social integration.

---

48 Kekaumenos (1998): 168. *Jus Graecoromanum*, ed. Zepos, 4:177.

49 *Actes d'Iviron*, 2:§§44 and 47. Lemerle, *Cinq études*, 15–63.

Conclusion

Slavery became the engine for new social and political structures necessary for the formation of medieval societies. We are now far from the late Roman empire where slavery served as a tool in the management and control of urban markets. Instead, slavery created new types of wealth and power that necessitated relations of personal control and dependency, in short: private subjects. Notwithstanding the differences in polities, structures, organizations, and beliefs, all these medieval societies used slavery to create private subjects, for various reasons. The management of businesses, private enterprises, households, families, and armies was dependent on personal ties of dependency which slavery provided. Slaves were certainly not the only labour force, and probably not even the biggest. Yet, slavery offered something unique: versatility that was easily controlled and managed by private and public forces thanks to the fact that its definitions were flexible and could be manipulated by public and private powers alike. In the following chapter we will see that religion played a role in making the institution of slavery even more versatile. Conversion of the enslaved to the religion of the enslaver was both a way of establishing a personal relationship between enslaver and enslaved and constituting the enslaved as a subject of the enslaver by incorporating the enslaved into the "society of believers," whether of Christians, Muslims, or Jews.

In *The Problem of Slavery as History*, Joseph Miller understood the idea of slavery as an institution, in conflict with its perception as a historical process. For him, slavery as a historical process meant simply a means for private enslavers to react to changes in current circumstances. Yet, tracing the role that slaveries played in the formations of medieval societies reveals slavery to be a historical process precisely because its institutionalization was in constant flux and could adapt to changing circumstances. Thanks to its fluid definitions it offered conditions for social and political developments. The two perceptions of slavery, as social institution and as historical process, therefore, are not in conflict. Rather, the first enables the second.

Chapter 5

Migration, Integration, Connectivity

Ninth to Eleventh Centuries

In the previous chapter we saw different uses medieval societies made of enslaved people. Slavery became important in
institutionalizing personal forms of control that sustained the
social, economic, and also the political system of medieval
societies and contributed to their development. The medieval world systematized enslavement in different ways and
for different ends. We examined specific and localized forms
of enslavement, but also revealed their common traits. The
enslaved were employed in diverse, versatile, and flexible
ways. The adaptability of forms of enslavement to changing
circumstances made it useful for social change. The result
were distinct medieval forms of slavery, fundamental to the
social structure, system, and organization of medieval societies. Social dynamics had become dependent on forms of
enslavement. This is why we understand slavery as a historical process and why we refer to it using the plural form.

And yet, medieval economies, societies, and cultures
were connected. The question of connectivity is all the more
pertinent because medieval slaveries depended on the
enslavement of foreigners and their integration as dominated
subjects. How did these systems of migration and integration function? How did they connect one to another despite
being distinct and diverse? The present chapter develops a
global perspective in order to complete the local perspective
adopted in the previous chapter. It explores the ways in which
medieval slaveries formed a coherent system that connected

societies, economies, and polities. Slavery proves to be a historical process also in its role as a means of connectivity. But this role cannot be examined without taking into account the fact that the enslaved did not play this role out of free will. Human beings who were kidnapped, coerced, and trafficked found themselves forcibly migrated away from their homes and families. The role of slavery as a historical process in the development of the societies of the first millennium was carried out on the back of its victims, enslaved women, men, and children. How can we begin to grasp slavery from their point of view? As we shall see, perceiving the enslaved as coerced migrants, forcibly dislocated, trafficked, and integrated into an enslaving environment will help us to study the terrible psychological impact of the system of slavery.

The slave trade, forced migration, coercion, and human trafficking have all played a terrible role in the long history of humanity. These phenomena connected societies, economies, and polities by using enslavement, trading of humans, and forced migration, that is, migration which otherwise would not have happened. The link between enslavement and migration is shared by scholars who today reexamine the history and the effects of the transatlantic slave trade.[1] Atlantic slavery is by far the best and most appallingly documented phenomenon of forced migration in the world's history. Although more than eleven million enslaved Africans reached the Americas between the sixteenth and nineteenth centuries (with over two million Africans dying on the way), scholarship has tended to differentiate between slavery and migration as two different phenomena that created modern American

---

1 Rhonda V. Magee, "Slavery as Immigration?," *University of San Francisco Law Review* 44 (2009): 273–95. Shannon E. Clancy, "Immigration and Modern Slavery: How the Laws of One Fail to Provide Justice to the Victims of the Other," *University of Baltimore Law Review* 46, no. 2 (2017): 335–52. Daromir Rudnyckyj, "Technologies of Servitude: Governmentality and Indonesian Transnational Labor Migration," *Anthropological Quarterly* 77, no. 3 (2004): 407–34. Wim Klooster, *Migration, Trade, and Slavery in an Expanding World: Essays in Honor of Pieter Emmer* (Leiden: Brill, 2009).

societies.[2] Migration was mostly perceived as a voluntary act. In contrast, the objective of the Atlantic slave trade was the exploitation of enslaved Africans. The rationale was economic, human trafficking on a grandiose scale, the abduction and forced displacement of Africans as merchandise within and out of Africa being the means to attain these objectives.

Today, however, this perspective is challenged by scholars who consider forced migration as part of slavery and slavery as a form of migration, enforced on the migrants by coercion.[3] Such studies do not intend to change the historical perspective of Atlantic slavery, but to develop alongside it a new perspective in which slavery will take its place in the history of migration to the Americas.[4] This can lead to analogies between the transatlantic slave trade and modern trafficking in humans (Bravo, "Exploring the Analogy"). If we compare this to modern slavery and forced migration today, we will find it difficult to identify an intentionally programmed economic framework at their core. Yet, forms of trafficking in humans are also systematized today using coercion, displacement, deception, and smuggling (Shelley, *Human Trafficking*). They are also driven by forced displacement and forced migration which does not necessarily mean physical coercion (Bravo, "Exploring the Analogy"). The 2006 case of "The Queen v Wei Tang" (see "Introduction" above) where five women entered Australia following agreements they made with a broker in Thailand, and found themselves in debt bondage, is a clear indication that enslavement of migrants does not necessarily depend on their coercion. Social and legal circumstances can

---

2 Eltis, *The Rise of African Slavery in the Americas*. Joel Quirk and Darshan Vigneswaran, eds., *Slavery, Migration and Contemporary Bondage in Africa* (Trenton: Africa World, 2013).

3 See Damian A. Pargas, *Slavery and Forced Migration in the Antebellum South* (Cambridge: Cambridge University Press, 2014) for forced migration of slaves within the antebellum American South.

4 See O. Pétré-Grenouilleau, *Les traites négrières: Essai d'histoire globale* (Paris: Gallimard, 2004) for a global view on migration and enslavement of Africans to Asia and Europe.

lead to forced displacement and migration without actually physically coercing the migrants. What do we mean in fact by forced migration, and how is it connected to slavery as a historical process?

The term "forced migration" usually refers to people who are either coerced, pushed, or driven into migration by other people or by their living circumstances and conditions. The concepts "forced migration" and "free will" are therefore not always in contradiction. A human being can be pushed to migrate out of economic, political, or other circumstances in their life. The decision to migrate may be taken by the migrants themselves, but the result can lead them to be coerced or bound in a way that restrict their human and civil rights in relation to other members of the same society. Being able to make "free will" decisions therefore does not exclude being coerced, trafficked, or forcibly uprooted. In order not to contrast "free will" and "forced migration" scholars tend to use another concept: agency, that is, the ability to act upon one's independent decisions. This enables us to avoid the distinction between "forced" and "free," and to focus instead on a "passive" versus "active" field of action. In the case of "The Queen v Wei Tang," the five women exercised agency in entering Australia illegally and then in working to free themselves from their contracts which illegally bound them to their purchaser. The fact that they were enslaved by their purchaser did not diminish their agency. Agency can be an active response by an individual to a situation of severe exploitation. This puts forced migration, slavery, trafficking, and coercion together as extreme forms of human exploitation. It enables us to avoid concepts such as "free will," "freedom," and "unfreedom," and instead analyze and understand situations and circumstances that force people to migrate and make them vulnerable to severe exploitation and enslavement. In fact, "free will" and "freedom," prove to be relative terms which help very little in defining or identifying slavery.

This is the reason why scholars are struggling to find a coherent definition and common criteria that will enable us to understand migration and slavery as part of one system.[5] The main questions that scholars of forced migration are concerned with are therefore: firstly, what is its significance? Secondly, in what way is this related to or does it lead to enslavement? Medieval evidence proves extremely informative for both questions. The medieval world was composed of different societies, cultures, and economies, for which forced migration and enslavement formed a means of connectivity.

From Internal Forced Migration to International Human Trafficking

War, revolts, and conflict were the main causes of enslavement in the Roman Empire, supplemented by the enslavement of convicts and exposure of children and their enslavement. Forced migration of enslaved victims was common, but it mainly comprised internal migration, that is within the Roman Empire and its expanding territories.[6] Enslavement

---

5 J. O'Connell Davidson, "Troubling Freedom: Migration, Debt, and Modern Slavery," *Migration Studies* 13 (2013): 1–20. David A. Martin, T. A. Aleinikoff, H. Motomura, and M. Fullerton, *Forced Migration: Law and Policy* (Eagan: Thomason West, 2007; 2nd ed. in 2013). D. Turton, *Conceptualising Forced Migration*, Refugee Studies Centre Working Paper Series 12 (Oxford: Refugee Studies Centre, 2003) (available at www.rsc.ox.ac.uk/files/publications/working-paper-series/wp12-conceptualising-forced-migration-2003.pdf). Stephen Castles, "Towards a Sociology of Forced Migration and Social Transformation," *Sociology* 37, no. 1 (2003): 13–34. Pargas, *Slavery and Forced Migration in the Antebellum South.* "Symposium: The Evolving Definition of the Immigrant Worker: The Intersection between Employment, Labor, and Human Right Law," *University of San Francisco Law School* 253 (Fall 2009): https://www.law.berkeley.edu/files/thcsj/TheEEOCandImmigrantWorkers.pdf (accessed September 5, 2018).

6 Josephus, *The Jewish War*. Noy, *Jewish Inscriptions*, 1:§26. Rotman, "Captives and Redeeming Captives." Scheidel, "The Roman Slave Supply." Cf. *Digesta Justiniani*, D.39.4.16. Cosmas Indicopleustes, *Topographie chrétienne*, ed. and trans. Wanda Wolska-Conus, 3 vols. Paris: Cerf, 1968–1973). Procopius, *De bello Gothico*, bk. 4, ch. 3.

went hand in hand with other forms of domination as a way of annexing conquered populations. Similar dynamics of geopolitical expansion and social control were also used in the early Caliphate to form the Muslim-Arab elite. Slavery relied on the enslavement of captives. Wars and conquests filled this demand. But by the end of the eighth century the geopolitical map stabilized. It was no longer a period of large conquests and geopolitical annexations. Piracy, captivity, abduction, and enslavement of people, present already in the fifth to eighth centuries, became the dominant forms of enslavement especially in frontier zones. This corresponded to the Viking Age (800–1030) which was marked by continuous raiding across Northern Europe, settlement, and expansion of Scandinavian influence. In the south, the rich Mediterranean and Near-Eastern societies depended on the importation of enslaved people. Human trafficking served as the main way to enslave these people, merchandise them, and sell them. This was a global phenomenon of forced migration. The victims were forcibly uprooted from their homeland, abducted, enslaved, trafficked, and sold far from home and country.[7]

This destiny was not limited to inhabitants of frontier zones. It grew into an international commercial map of forced migration. Sub-Saharan Africans, Slavs and Bulgars from Eastern Europe, Turks from the Steppes and other inhabitants of the Caucasus, as well as people from the British Isles were enslaved, trafficked, and sold from Iberia to Iraq and from the sub-Sahara to Scandinavia. This necessitated an international network of trade in humans, which was a creation of the Central Middle Ages (Rotman, "The Map of the Medieval Slave Trade"). It linked the different medieval societies with peripheral regions. Abduction, enslavement, trafficking, and migration were the engine that created this network. And the form of war changed too.

---

7 Charles Verlinden, *L'Esclavage dans l'Europe médiévale*, 2 vols. (Brugge and Gent: De Tempel and Rijksuniversiteit, 1955 and 1977). Rotman, *Byzantine Slavery and the Mediterranean World*. McCormick, *Origins of the European Economy*.

From Local to Global

We begin to see, from the eighth century, military campaigns where total defeat of the enemy was no longer the principal military objective. Raids and piracy by naval and land forces became frequent. The aim of both was humans who could be enslaved and sold in foreign lands. Piracy, particularly, proved to be a very effective way for procuring slaves. It became prevalent in the Eastern Mediterranean during the central medieval period.[8] It was adopted as a military strategy in both the Caliphate and Byzantium and became most disturbing for the Mediterranean population in the ninth to tenth centuries. Sicily and Crete, for example, were used as bases for raids on Byzantine coastal communities. Muslim pirates threatened the Greek islands, Southern Italy, the Peloponnese, and the coasts of Greece and Asia Minor. The target was not military victory but the Byzantine population itself which was kidnapped, enslaved, and then sold in the markets of North Africa from Ifiqyia (modern Tunisia) to Egypt.[9] The Byzantines in turn launched military attacks on the Muslim population in the Eastern Mediterranean.[10] So, enslavement and forced migration of enslaved foreigners became a common Mediterranean practice. Religion was the criterion that determined who was a foreigner and who was not. The first could be enslaved, the second could not.

Christians and Jews were raided by Muslims, enslaved, and sold across the various caliphates and emirates. Since the ninth century the Islamic world no longer comprised one

---

8 Youval Rotman, "Medieval Slavery in a New Geopolitical Space," in *Critical Readings on Global Slavery*, ed. D. Alan Pargas and F. Roşu (Leiden: Brill, 2017), 588–664 (https://doi.org/10.1163/9789004346611_022).

9 One characteristic example: *Vita di Sant'Elia il Giovane*, ed. G. Rossi Taibbi (Palermo: Istituto siciliano di studi bizantini e neoellenici, 1962). Ibn 'Idhārī, *Kitāb al-bayān al-mughrib*, 1:64.

10 *The Taktika of Leo VI*, ed. and trans. G. T. Dennis (Washington, DC: Dumbarton Oaks, 2010), 384–86. Rotman, "Medieval Slavery in a New Geopolitical Space."

single political state but was divided between ruling dynasties of caliphates and emirates, the most influential being the Abbasids who ruled from Baghdad. The dynamics of enslavement and forced migration in the Mediterranean was a real threat to the life of the local population. In the Central Middle Ages it resulted in a new market for the ransoming of captives.[11] Special envoys as well as private agents managed to ransom captives and return them to their families and faith, mostly for a fee.[12] Jewish communities were particularly imaginative in creating an international inter-community network to ransom enslaved Jews, based on the religious precept of solidarity and shared destiny.[13] All this points to global medieval dynamics in which enslavement was a way to procure and coerce forced migrants. The result was a large movement of people between the different medieval societies.

The inhabitants of these societies were not the only victims of this movement. Other peoples were enslaved, uprooted, trafficked, and forcibly migrated far away from their homeland. These were people who lived beyond the borders of Mediterranean and Near Eastern societies, who were pagans up until the Central Middle Ages. Ransom was not an option for them. Unlike Christian, Muslim, and Jewish believers, they had no religion to maintain their status as free born and no fellow believers to take measures to preserve their freedom. They were enslaved and traded, often by the local leaders and

---

11 Youval Rotman, "Byzantium and the International Slave Trade in the Central Middle Ages," in *Trade in Byzantium: Papers from the Third International Sevgi Gönül Byzantine Studies Symposium*, ed. N. Necipoglu and Paul Magdalino (Istanbul: Koç University Publications, 2016), 129–42.

12 *Actes d'Iviron*, 1:§16. *The Life of St. Nikon*, ed. D. F. Sullivan (Brookline: Hellenic College Press, 1987), ch. 70.

13 Jacob Mann, *The Jews in Egypt and in Palestine under the Fāṭimid Caliphs*, 2 vols. (orig. publ. 1920–1922; Oxford: Oxford University Press, 1969): 1:87–90; 2:344–65. Jacob Mann, *Texts and Studies in Jewish History and Literature*, 2 vols. (Cincinnati: Hebrew Union College Press, 1931–1935), 1:367–70.

chieftains of regions where in the ninth to eleventh centuries no stable organized form of government existed.

Medieval descriptions by historians, geographers, or voyagers as well as correspondence, fiscal documents, and political treaties, along with archaeological findings enable us to change a regional Mediterranean perspective into a global medieval one that includes peoples who were the main source of slaves in the central medieval period (McCormick, *Origins of the European Economy*). In the sixth to seventh centuries enslavement of free born inhabitants was not uncommon in Western Europe and enslaved people, including children, were traded from Anglo-Saxon England and the Frankish Empire to the Mediterranean. In the ninth and tenth centuries slave traders turned their focus to the northeast onto the pagan population of Eastern Europe. The three main rivers—the Dnieper, Don, and Volga—connected the North European hinterlands to the Black Sea and Caspian Sea. The markets in the Middle East from Constantinople to Baghdad were connected along these routes by Rus' and Viking ("Varangians" in Greek) traders, who brought their victims to the markets on the Black Sea and the Khazar main port on the Volga delta: Itil/Atil.

The Vikings in particular were prominent raiders in both Eastern and Western Europe, abducting, enslaving, and selling the local population. Their activities are recorded in Latin, Greek, and Arabic sources of the period. Most of the routes they took were fluvial and maritime. Their victims were sold to foreign slave traders, but sometimes also enslaved by Viking tribes in Iceland, Gotland, or Sweden, where they were used in the retinue of the elite as well as in tribal households.[14] Burials alongside a deceased Scandinavian of the enslaved, mutilated or decapitated, suggests a pagan custom

---

14 Ben Raffield, "The Slave Markets of the Viking World: Comparative Perspectives on an 'Invisible Archaeology,'" *Slavery and Abolition* 40, no. 4 (2019): 682–705. Karras, *Slavery and Society in Medieval Scandinavia*.

of grave gifts in which the enslaved was buried to accompany the enslaver into the afterlife.[15]

Michael McCormick in his *Origins of the European Economy* attributed a key role to the international slave market in the transfer of goods, people, and money between the northern and southern Mediterranean coasts. In this trade Eastern Europe proved to be a major source of slaves for Mediterranean societies, and for Byzantium and the Caliphate in particular. Both were the richest markets available. The people to their north, from Britain to the Urals, did not mint gold or silver coins and so this made these regions dependent on Byzantium and the caliphates for the supply of precious metals. Indeed, hoards containing Byzantine and Arab coins from the ninth and particularly tenth centuries have been excavated in Eastern and Northern Europe.[16] They point to a large trade in gold and silver from the Mediterranean southeast to the European and Eurasian north.

What could European societies trade in return for these metals? Along with furs, wax, and weapons they traded humans. Iron shackles, chains, and collars used on humans, found in archaeological excavations in Eastern and Northern Europe as well as in the British Isles are a terrible witness to the extent of medieval human trafficking.[17] We are still not well informed on who exactly the victims were. However, descriptions of pirate and merchant raiders who controlled

---

15 E. Naumann et al. "Slaves as Burial Gifts in Viking Age Norway? Evidence from Stable Isotope and Ancient DNA Analyses," *Journal of Archaeological Science* 41 (2014): 533–40.

16 See fig. 1 from M. Jankowiak, "Dirhams for Slaves. Investigating the Slavic Slave Trade in the Tenth Century," lecture delivered at All Souls, Oxford in 2012: https://www.academia.edu/1764468/Dirhams_for_slaves_Investigating_the_Slavic_slave_trade_in_the_tenth_century (accessed March 17, 2021).

17 A summary of the archaeological evidence and critics on its interpretation: Janel M. Fontaine, "Early Medieval Slave-Trading in the Archaeological Record: Comparative Methodologies," *Early Medieval Europe* 25, no. 4 (2017): 466–88.

the movement of people from Dublin (a Viking settlement in the ninth century) to the Volga and enslaved passengers are common.[18] In fact, no real distinction existed between pirates, slave traders, and merchants in the medieval world. Pirates were merchants, and their activities, devastating for the local population of Eastern Europe, were supplemented by raids on local tribes who sold their kidnapped victims to foreign slave traders.

A similar picture is visible from the descriptions of Muslim geographers and historians who describe medieval routes through their own voyages. Ibn Faḍlān describes his voyage from Baghdad to the Bulgar Khanate along the Volga in 922, where he met Rus' raiders on the Volga who were trading in furs, wax, and slaves. Rus' traders were also present in the Black Sea. Their targets were the Byzantine and Abbasid markets: both Constantinople and Samarra had large slave markets.[19] The three river routes—the Dnieper, Don, and Volga—were part of a much larger map of the medieval slave trade (Rotman, "The Map of the Medieval Slave Trade"). The Vikings used both the sea and rivers to journey from the Baltic into Eastern Europe and across the North Sea to the British Isles and Normandy. Other routes led from Eastern Europe to the Western Mediterranean through Central and Western Europe. Here too, rivers were the main routes, the Danube and the Rhone in particular. The destinations of these routes were the ports of Italy and the south of France, where slave traders from further south embarked: Venetians, Amalfitanians, Muslims, and Jews. These bought the abducted Eastern European people and sold them to the Mediterranean markets from Islamic Iberia to the Middle East. A western Viking

---

18 Poul Holm, "The Slave Trade of Dublin, Ninth to Twelfth Centuries," *Peritia* 5 (1988): 317–45.

19 *Accounts of Medieval Constantinople: The* Patria, trans. Albrecht Berger (Cambridge, MA: Harvard University Press, 2013), 94 (bk. 2, ch. 64). Aḥmad ibn Yaḥyā Balādhurī, *Liber expugnationis regionum / Kitāb futūḥ al-buldān*, ed. M. J. de Goeje (Leiden: Brill, 1892), vii.258–263, which is translated and available online.

route linked the Baltic with al-Andalus through Gascony and across the Pyrenees.

North to south traffic across Europe left traces in languages. Although not all European slaves were of Slavic origin, in Byzantium, the Umayyad Caliphate of Iberia, and North Africa, the term "Slavs" (Greek: *sklavoi*, Arabic: *ṣaḳāliba*) became a synonym for European slaves in general. In al-Andalus it denoted qualified enslaved eunuchs (Meouak, *Ṣaqâliba*). The term entered other non-Slavic European languages (*slave, esclave, Sklave, schiavo, sklavos, slav, sclav, slaaf, esclavo, escravo*).

The Eurasian slave trade that connected the northeast of Europe to the Mediterranean South and the Viking slave trade from the British Isles, is not the whole picture. The Mediterranean and Middle Eastern markets also imported humans from the Sahel and sub-Saharan Africa. Here too, medieval Muslim historians and geographers provide the main evidence. From the late seventh century and more so in the eighth and ninth centuries when the population of North Africa became predominantly Muslim, Arab slave traders turned to the Berber people of North Africa and the commercial centres in the Sahel to procure Africans. Through the Saharan towns from Sijilmassa (in modernday Morocco), Ouragla (south Algeria) to Ghat, Ghadames, and Zawila in Fezzan (Saharan Libya), and Kaouar (Niger), a network of trade routes connected the Sahel and sub-Saharan Africa to the markets of North Africa: Tlemcen and Tiaret/Tahert in today's Algeria, Kairouan and Sfax in today's Tunisia, and Tripoli in Libya.[20] In East Africa the

---

20 Ibn Ḥawḳal, *La configuration de la Terre*, 1:80–92. al-Bakrī, *Kitāb al masālik wa-l-mamālik*, ed. A. van Leeuwen and André Ferré, 2 vols. (Tunis: al-Dār al-'arabiyya li-l-kitāb, 1992), 2:833–94. Trabelsi, "Commerce et esclavage dans le Maghreb oriental." Mohamed Meouak, "Esclaves et métaux précieux de l'Afrique subsaharienne vers le maghreb au moyen âge à la lumière des sources arabes," *Historia Medieval* 23 (2010): 113–34 and Meouak, "Esclaves noirs et esclaves blancs en al-Andalus umayyade et en Ifrīqiya fāṭimide," in *Couleurs de l'esclavage sur les deux rives de la Méditerranée (Moyen Age–XXᵉ siècle)*, ed. R. Botte and A. Stella (Paris: Karthala, 2012),

slave trade connected Nubia and Ethiopia to the port of Zeyla (Saylac in Somalia) on the Gulf of Aden,[21] and the Kanem region (modernday Chad) and the Sudan (literally "the [land of the] Blacks") to the Mediterranean markets of North Africa from Kairouan to Egypt, and from there westward to Islamic Iberia and eastward to Iraq. The ninth-century geographer al-Yaʿḳūbī describes this trans-Saharan trafficking:

> "Beyond Waddan to the south is the town of Zawila. Its people are Muslims, all of them Ibāḍiyya, and go on pilgrimage to Mecca [...]. They export black slaves from among the Miriyyūn, the Zaghawiyyūn, the Marwiyyūn and from other peoples of the Sudan, because they live close to Zawila, whose people capture them [...]. The kings of the Sudan sell their people without any pretext of war [...]. Zawila (South Libya) is a land of date palms, where sorghum and other grains are sown. Various people live there from Khurasan, al-Basra and al-Kufa. Fifteen days' journey beyond Zawila is a town called Kaouar (North-East Niger), inhabited by Muslims from various tribes, most of them Berbers. It is they who bring in the Blacks [slaves] (as-Sūdān)."[22]

The routes that were used to trade enslaved Africans from south of the Sahara to North Africa were part of an international network of trade routes that connected the Mediterranean markets of North Africa to southern Europe and from western Europe to the Near East (Egypt, Syria, and Iraq). A detailed description of routes that connected the Western

---

25–53. Jelle Bruning, "Slave Trade Dynamics in Abbasid Egypt: The Papyrological Evidence," *Journal of the Economic and Social History of the Orient* 63, no. 5–6 (2020): 682–742. Savage, "Berbers and Blacks."

21 al-Muḳaddasī, *Aḥsan al-taqāsīm fī maʿrifat al-āqālīm*, ed. Michael Jan de Goeje (Leiden: Brill, 1906), 241. Power, *The Red Sea from Byzantium to the Caliphate*.

22 J. F. P. Hopkins and N. Levtzion, eds., *Corpus of Early Arabic Sources for West African History* (Cambridge: Cambridge University Press, 1981), 22. Cf. the Beja/Bādja's raids on the tribes Ḳift, Ḳus, and Aswan: Ibn Ḥawḳal, *La configuration de la Terre*, 1:51–52.

Mediterranean to the Near East and onto the Far East is given by another ninth-century geographer, Ibn Khurradādhbih.[23] He describes in detail the activities of Jewish merchants named *al-Rādhāniyya* who speak Arabic, Persian, Greek, and Slavonic among other languages, and trade in slaves (among them eunuchs), silk brocade, furs, swords, and spices. Their four international routes connected the ports of southern Europe to North Africa, the Near East, Byzantium, and continued further eastward to Sind and India from where they imported spices back to the Mediterranean markets (see Rotman, "The Map of the Medieval Slave Trade").

The fact that these traders were Jews need not surprise us. As a discriminated-against religious minority Jews were constrained from buying slaves in Christian and Muslim countries, and were limited in their ability to convert their slaves to Judaism. They relied heavily on the international slave trade. Indeed, letters from this period of Jewish merchants discovered in the medieval synagogue of old Cairo (the Cairo Genizah) attest to their using slaves as commercial agents from Sicily through Yemen to India (Goitein, *Letters of Medieval Jewish Traders*). Yet, the fact that Jews were involved in the slave trade was also met with severe criticism. In the Latin West, ecclesiastical writers expressed their opposition to selling Christian slaves and slaves in general to Jewish and Muslim traders.[24] Their writings were met with international agreements between Byzantium and Venice which forbad the collaboration with traders in slaves and arms from Muslim lands.[25]

---

23 Ibn Khurradādhbih, *Kitb al-Maslik wa-al-mamlik / Liber viarum et regnorum*, ed. M. J. de Goeje (repr. 1967; Leiden: Brill, 1889), 152–55.

24 Agobard of Lyon, *Opera omnia*, ed. L. van Acker (Turnhout: Brepols, 1981), §§6 and 11. Gregory the Great, *Registrum epistularum*, bk. 3, no. 37.

25 G. L. F. Tafel and G. M. Thomas, eds., *Urkunden zur älteren Handels- und Staatsgeschichte der Republik Venedig*, 3 vols. (orig. 1856–1857; Amsterdam: Hakkert, 1964) 1:5; 1:16–17. *I trattati con Bisanzio 992–1198*, ed. M. Pozza and G. Ravegnani, Pacta Veneta 4 (Venice: Il Cardo, 1993), §1.

Such strong reaction reveals the religious factor that underlay the medieval slave trade, and pushed the traders and enslavers further to the peripheries of their known world. This explains the extent of the slave trade in Africa and also in pagan Eastern Europe. If in the ninth century the Rus' were selling the local Slavs into the slave markets of Byzantium and the Caliphate, by the end of the century when their elite became Christian, they adopted the Byzantine perspective that prohibited the enslavement of fellow believers. The treaties that Byzantium signed with the Rus' in the tenth century reveal a joint front against the enslavement of members of both polities.[26] Nevertheless, Rus' traders still supplied enslaved people to Byzantium and the Abbasid Caliphate, but procured further to the East. In other words, the expansion of monotheism beyond the Mediterranean and the Near East, oriented the slave trade towards the pagan populations that were found further and further to the European northeast and sub-Saharan South. There was a global economic rationale to this trading network.

The Global Economic Rationale to the Medieval Slave Trade

Human beings were expensive. Prices of European male slaves varied from twenty gold coins in Constantinople to thirty-three gold dinars in Egypt and Syria. The difference in price marks the difference in trade routes. The price of an enslaved woman in Egypt could reach thirty dinars. These were extremely high prices in comparison to other types of merchandise, undoubtedly due to the long itineraries involved in their acquisition.

While Greek sources refer to the origin of the enslaved by topo-ethnic terms ("Bulgars," "Scythians," and *sklavoi* for Slavs), Arabic trade documents mostly specify their origin by colour: "yellow" probably for North Africans or Nubians,

---

26 I. Sorlin, "Les traités de Byzance avec la Russie au Xe siècle," *Cahiers du Monde russe et soviétique* 2, nos. 3–4 (1962): 313–60 and 447–75).

"black" (Arabic: *Sūdān*) for sub-Saharan Africans, and "white" or "red" for Europeans. Slaves of European origin were more expensive in the Islamic world than African slaves, probably because of the longer routes, complex trade networks, and taxes. Customs and tolls existed all along these routes and turned the slave trade into a profitable business for local authorities. In this way, the slave trade represented an international forced movement of people and domination, but was also a means of connecting economies.

Since medieval human trafficking was determined by religion and relied on importing pagan populations via long and expensive routes, it formed an international commercial nexus. The entire commercial dynamics of this slave trade depended on coercion and trafficking in humans from less developed economies in the northeast (Eastern Europe, the Steppes, the Caucasus), northwestern Europe (from the Baltic to the British Isles), and sub-Saharan Africa. It allowed these less developed economies to connect with the richer societies in a global interchange of wealth. In this sense, human merchandising was a means, even the main means, for the development of less advanced economies. The Vikings, the Rus', the Khazars, and the Bulgar Khanate of the Volga advanced their economies and governmental organization by using trade in humans. The elites of both the Rus' of Kiev and the Khazars converted in the ninth century, the first adopted Christianity which subordinated them to the Byzantine Church, the khanate elite of the latter converted to Judaism. The Christianization of Scandinavian chieftains has also begun in the same period.

The same is also true for the commercial markets of the Sahel whose economic success was determined by the role they played in the trafficking of Africans from south of the Sahara to markets from al-Andalus to Iraq. Here too, the economic expansion of the slave trade went hand in hand with the conversion of these regions to Islam. In other words, the slave trade and the demand for slaves was used by peripheral societies to connect to wealthier societies and advance their own economies at the expanse of enslaved pagans. The forced migration of the victims of this dynamic produces a redistribution of wealth from more to less advanced economies. Migration was the means to create a global economic map of exchanges. Humans were the most profitable merchandise that underdeveloped economies could offer to participate in this network. They were the most numerous and expensive element in this international trade. Their migration became essential for underdeveloped economies to participate in global trade. The violent, cruel, forced migration of the enslaved made up the key financial element of international trade at this period. It facilitated the development of less advanced medieval economies and the geopolitical and economic expansion of the medieval world. If we consider medieval slaveries within the framework of forced migration, and the enslaved as medieval migrants, let us now turn to see how they integrated into their destination economies. What might the picture look like from the viewpoint of the enslaved migrants?

Integration of the Enslaved

It is impossible to estimate the number of men, women, and children who were enslaved, trafficked, and forced into a life far from their home, people, and family in the Middle Ages. Unlike the Atlantic slave trade we have little concrete numerical evidence before the early modern period. However, societies which had the means to acquire foreigners did so, and on a large scale. Migration and forms of enslavement prove to be in the Middle Ages two sides of the same coin. Enslavement depended on forced migration to foster economic expansion, while forced migration depended on slave markets and the demand for the enslaved. As we saw above religion determined these activities and oriented them towards the pagan populations of northern Europe, the Steppes, and sub-Saharan Africa, while using transnational routes that spread across central and southern Europe, the North Sea, Mesopotamia, across the Sahara and the Mediterranean. Religion also played an important role in the sociocultural integration of the enslaved forced migrants, through their conversion to the faith and social order of their owners whether Christian, Muslim, or Jewish.

This analysis is entirely based on evidence that were left by the enslavers, raiders, traffickers, and other agents. We have nearly no testimonies of the enslaved themselves, other than stories and acts of self-sale mostly from Latin Western Europe and Byzantium (see chapter 3 above). Texts and private documents of the period from Christian, Muslim, and Jewish writers normally paint a gentle picture of an ideal household and depict the enslaved as fully integrated into the enslaver's family.[27] This picture should not deceive us. This was not a relationship of mutual dependency between enslaver and enslaved but was based on the commodifying of humans. The enslaver was dependent on the enslaved as a socioeconomic human investment for the benefit of his household's economy. The enslaved was completely dependent on the enslaver for everything else. The fact that the enslaved were migrants made their dependency all the more complete.

Nevertheless, merchandised humans were also treated as humans, especially because they were valuable and were not readily disposed of. Testaments of well-to-do people, and other private legal documents reveal a social mentality in which the enslaved was considered part of the enslaver's family (Rotman, *Byzantine Slavery and the Mediterranean World*). Sometimes this led to marriage, adoption, manumission, and inheritance. Integration of the enslaved was certainly an objective of the enslaver, but the enslaved never became the equal of the enslaver. On the contrary, the main purpose of integration was to render the enslaved a subordinate dominated subject. Conversion of the enslaved to the enslaver's faith reinforced this. For this it was particularly important that the slaves were foreign infidel migrants.

---

27 Rotman, *Byzantine Slavery and the Mediterranean World*. Lemerle, *Cinq études*, 15–63. Gertrude Robinson, ed., *Cartulary of the Greek Monastery of St. Elias and St. Anastasius of Carbone*, 3 vols. in 1 (Rome: Institutum Orientalium Studiorum, 1928), iv.53; x.59; xi.61.

Pagans who were not firmly tied to an exclusive faith were more easily converted and integrated as "newcomers" to the society of believers. The conversion of the enslaved by the enslaver set a religious framework to the relationship of control between two persons and enabled the integration of the new believers to the new faith via their enslavers.

From Object to Believer: The Slave's Conversion

Conversion acted as a tool of inclusion of the "newcomers." It made the enslaved a believer and a member of the spiritual family of the enslaver. A famous converted slave was Bilāl ibn Rabāḥ of African origin, who became one of Muhammad's first followers in Mecca while still a slave of an idolater. Muhammad had him bought from the latter, manumitted, took him to Medina, and made him the first Muezzin. Another example is the story of Ṣafiyya, a married Jewess from Medina who was captured and enslaved in 628 by the Muslims. She converted to Islam and became Muhammad's wife.[28] In one of the Icelandic sagas the tenth-century Icelandic leader Olaf Hoskuldsson (Olaf the Peacock) is said to have been the son of Melkorka, an enslaved Irish woman who had been purchased and become the concubine of a Viking chieftain.[29] A Shiite tradition holds that the mother of the twelfth Shiite Imam al-Mahadi, the redeemer, was Narjis Mālika Wardās, a Byzantine princess who was captured, enslaved, and sold in Baghdad's slave market to Ḥasan ibn ʿAlī al-ʿAskarī (the eleventh Shiite Imam).[30] The Byzantine epic *Digenis Akritas* turns this *topos*

---

28 Ibn Hishām, *as-Sīra an-Nabawīyya*, ed. ʿUmar ʿAbd a-Salām Tadmurī, 4 vols. (Beirut: Dār al-Kitāb al-ʿArabī, 1987–90), 1: 339–40 and 3:178–79.

29 *Laxdæla saga*, trans. Magnus Magnusson and Hermann Pálsson (London: Penguin, 1969), 63 (ch. 12).

30 Hadi Taghavi, Ehsan Roohi, and Navid Karimi, "An Ignored Arabic Account of a Byzantine Royal Woman," *al-Masāq* 32, no. 2 (2019): 1–17.

on its head by narrating how a Byzantine maiden captured by a Muslim emir convinces him to marry her, convert to Christianity, and defect to Byzantium. There are similar Byzantine stories of enslaved foreigners who were Christianized and adopted into their enslaver's family. In Byzantium enslavers who baptized their slaves became their godfathers.[31] Conversion made the enslaved a faithful believer and therefore a trustworthy member of the household and a private subject. Each medieval society had its own sets of collective beliefs which were used to turn the enslaved from an object to a private subject.

Members of religious minorities in both Christian and Muslim countries could not hold slaves of the predominant religion and were restricted in their ability to convert slaves to their beliefs. In the Caliphate, conversion of the slave of a Jew or a Christian to Islam meant his immediate liberation, as was the case with conversion to Christianity of slaves of Jews in Byzantium where only Christians could enslave Christianized slaves. Turning persons into subjects by making them solely dependent on "masters," slavery, and other extreme forms of social dependency—such as that based on land tenure or personal legal arrangements—made possible enlarged private domination. This became common in Western Europe, Byzantium, and the Islamic world. Private domination involved restricting the freedom of the dependent, whether enslaved or not. In the Latin West the two forms of dependency became mingled, while in the Greek East and the Caliphates a clear legal definition distinguished between slavery and land tenure. Creating methods by which individuals could dominate others and creating private subjects by restricting their freedom was the engine for the social and political development of medieval societies and economies. Migration and social integration were forced on the enslaved who had no say in either matter.

---

31 *Ecloga: Das Gesetzbuch Leons III. und Konstantinos' V*, ed. Ludwig Burgmann (Frankfurt: Lowenklau-Gesellschaft, 1982), 8.1.4. *Jus Graecoromanum*, ed. Zepos, 2:139.

Yet, this "religious factor" in the integration of the enslaved had another result: it changed their position dramatically. Becoming a believer made the enslaved also a subject of God and a fellow believer. Having a religious identity meant having a legal status. And this turned the enslaved from object into subject. One of the most interesting characteristics of the status of the enslaved in the medieval world was their increasing access to the law. Detectable already in Late Antiquity, it became more common in the medieval period thanks to the religious identity of the enslaved. Their religious and legal persona enabled the enslaved to exert their religious status—to marry, have a family, be loyal to God—and also act independently in order to attain freedom (Rotman, *Byzantine Slavery and the Mediterranean World*). So, although they were normally acquired to improve the economic position of their enslaver's household, the enslaved had agency and sometimes found the means (both legally and illegally) to become independent, sometimes even in accord with the enslaver's objectives. Religious belonging made them into faithful members of society and changed attitudes towards them. But here too, we struggle for evidence from the viewpoint of the enslaved.

Religion and Psychology: The Slave as a Person

How can we get into the point of view, mindset, or psychology of the enslaved victims? Perceiving them as forced migrants, abducted, coerced, and forcibly integrated into the enslaving environment helps us to see the mental suffering that sustained the global medieval system of slavery. Although we have no autobiographies by the enslaved themselves, we can still examine the way medieval literature presents their lived experiences and how their situation is portrayed. For this we have abundant literary sources. Most of them are presented as true stories about famous persons who were enslaved, although they are far from historical records. Nevertheless, by the themes they address and the situations they describe we can understand the connection between mentality, psychology, and reality in the Middle Ages. Indeed, the literary figure of the enslaved became prominent in medieval literature, and enslavement as human experience became itself a literary theme.

The story of St. Patrick's capture from his home in Britain by pirates and St. Jerome's *The Life of Malchus the Captive* reflect the reality of raids and enslavement in the fourth to sixth centuries (see chapter 3). The *topos* of the enslaved captive, victim of raids by slave traders, became one of the most popular themes of medieval literature in the ninth to eleventh centuries, especially in stories set within a Mediterranean environment. We have abundant stories, in Greek, Arabic, and Hebrew, of a captured figure as protagonist (Rotman, *Byzantine Slavery and the Mediterranean World*). If in Greco-Roman Antiquity stories that included enslaved figures usually portrayed them as objects, devoid of their own thoughts and actions, or use them to create comic situations (Fitzgerald, *Slavery and the Roman Literary Imagination*), this was no longer the case in the medieval period, where too many people found themselves enslaved victims. In this way, medieval literature adapted itself to everyday life, and writers responded to the questions and troubles of their time. The story of a person abducted through raids, enslaved, and trafficked to another country, then sold to a local, became recurrent in the central medieval period. The result was the *topos* of the enslaved captive, for whom enslavement is a mission, an ordeal, a quest, and even a road to sainthood. This is for example the story of St. Elias the Younger of Enna in Sicily, the *Vita di Sant'Elia il Giovane*. A revelation in childhood prefigured his captivity, enslavement, and a life of Christian mission. The prophecy was fulfilled when as a boy he was captured twice by Arab pirates. He was rescued the first time, but then trafficked to Ifriqiya (modern Tunisia) on the second occasion, where he got sold to a rich local Christian and became a key figure in his household. He regained his freedom and embarked on a religious mission to Muslim lands that brought him to the Holy Land, where he became a monk. After a voyage from Egypt to Syria he returned to southern

Italy. But en route to Constantinople he died in Thessaloniki and was buried in the monastery he founded in Calabria.

This is not a typical story of a victim of raids, trafficking, and enslavement in an enemy land. Elias is sold to a Christian, and so avoids having to convert to Islam, manages to get free, and finally returns to his homeland. Most enslaved victims of the period were not so lucky. However, this story is aimed precisely at them. It turns enslavement and forced migration into a destiny, a religious mission. The model is the biblical story of Joseph who was enslaved, trafficked, and sold in Egypt from where he rose and cleared the road to Egypt for the Sons of Israel. Indeed, the enslavement and forced migration of Joseph was explicitly used as a literary model in this period by Jewish, Christian, and Muslim writers alike (Rotman, *Byzantine Slavery and the Mediterranean World*). Moreover, by building on this narrative form, the writers presented an innovation: slavery and its misfortunes were portrayed from the point of view of the enslaved. This change of perspective went hand in hand with the recognition that the slaves were fellow believers.

Yet, this literature does not develop an abolitionist approach. Despite the terrible condition of the enslaved migrants, we do not find anything that resembles *Uncle Tom's Cabin*. Published in 1852 by Harriet Beecher Stowe (apparently inspired by the autobiographical *Life of Josiah Henson*) this novel epitomizes the role of literature in changing people's mentality towards unjust social phenomena. The narrative from the slave's point of view made readers identify with the reality of being a slave, an identification which led to a mental shift and eventually to political change. It was the culmination of a long literary tradition going back to the seventeenth century (see, for instance, *Amazing Grace: An Anthology of Poems About Slavery, 1660–1810*, ed. James G. Basker, in 2012) which undoubtedly influenced the abolitionist movement.

Medieval literature that treated slavery and presented it from the slave's point of view does not reveal similar attitudes that could lead to an abolitionist movement. On the contrary, the choice of the biblical enslavement of Joseph precludes it. Enslavement was portrayed instead as part of the divine plan that puts the enslaved believer to trial.

Enslaved Migrants and Racism

We have seen how conversion made enslaved foreigners into believers, coreligionists, and subjects. Counterbalancing this integrative tendency, we see other way to justify their enslavement and subjugation. This involved attributing "characters" and "qualities" to the "origin," "ethnicity," "colour," and "faith" of the enslaved. Constructing such traits for the enslaved, the foreigner, the migrant, have supported and sustained systems of slavery throughout history. They enable enslavers to develop an ideological framework to justify exploitation, trafficking, and enslavement. In eleventh-century Baghdad the Christian Iraqi physician Ibn Buṭlān described this in his treatise "Introduction to the Art of Making Good Purchases of Slaves." He combines proto-racism, pro-slavery, misogyny, and objectification of women into an ideological framework that connects migration and enslavement, and justifies this connection in a disturbing way:

"Indian women are meek and mild but they rapidly fade away. They are excellent breeders of children. They have one advantage over other women: It is said 'On divorce they become virgins again.' The men are good house-managers and experts in fine handicrafts, but they are apt to die from apoplexy at an early age. They are mostly brought from Qandahar. The women of Sind are noted for slim waist and long hair. The woman of Medina combines suavity and grace with coquetry and humor. She is neither jealous nor bad-tempered nor quarrelsome. She makes an excellent songstress. The Meccan woman is delicate, has small ankles and wrists and languishing eyes [...]. The Berber woman is unrivalled for breeding. Pliant to a degree, she accommodates herself to every kind of work [...]. According to the broker, Abu 'Othman, the ideal slave is a Berber girl who is exported out of her country at the age of nine, who spends three years at Medina and three at Mecca and at sixteen comes to Mesopotamia to be trained in elegant accomplishments. And, so, when sold at twenty-five, she unites, with her fine racial excellences, the coquetry of a Medinan, the delicacy of the Meccan, and the culture of the Mesopotamian woman [...]. At the markets blacks were much in evidence; the darker the uglier and the more pointed their teeth. They are not up to much. They are fickle and careless. Dancing and beating time are engrained in their nature. They say: were the black to fall from heaven to the earth he would beat time in falling. They have the whitest teeth and this because they have much saliva. Unpleasant is the smell emitted from their armpits and coarse is their skin. The Abyssinian woman, on the other hand, is weak and flabby and frequently suffers from consumption. She is ill-suited for song and dance and languishes in a foreign country. She is reliable and has a strong character in a feeble body. The women of Beja/Bādja/Bujjah (between Abyssinia and Nubia) have golden complexion, comely countenance, delicate skin, but an unlovely figure. They must be taken out of their country before circumcision, for often it is done so clumsily that the bones become visible. The men are brave but are prone to steal and so, they should not be trusted with money. And for this reason, precisely, they make bad house managers. Of all the blacks, the Nubian woman is the most adaptable and cheerful. Egypt agrees with her, for as at home she drinks the Nile water there too. Elsewhere she is liable to the diseases of the blood [...]. Fair skinned, the Turkish women are full of grace and animation. Their eyes are small but enticing. They are thick-set and are inclined to be of short stature. There are very few tall women among them. They are prolific in breeding and their offspring are but rarely ugly. They are never bad riders. They are generous; they are clean in their habits; they cook well; but they are unreliable [...]. The Greek woman is of red-white complexion, has smooth hair and blue eyes. She is obedient, and adaptable, well meaning, faithful and trustworthy. The men are useful as house managers, because of their love of order and disinclination to extravagance. Not infrequently they are well-trained in some fine handicraft. The Armenian is the worst of the white [...]. They are well-built, but have ugly feet. Chastity is unknown and theft is rampant among them. But they know not avarice. Coarse is their nature and coarse their speech. Let an Armenian slave be an hour without work and he will get into mischief. He only works under the threat of the cane or the stress of fear. When you find him lazy it is simply because he delights in laziness and not because he does not feel equal to work. You must then take to the cane, chastise him and make him do what you want."[32]

"Origin," "ethnicity," "colour," and "faith" are all cultural constructs used to create sociocultural distinctions between humans in a proto-racist manner. They provided justifications to sustain and support the medieval systems of subjugation, control, and enslavement. Such cultural and ideological constructs of proto-racism were not new. Medieval societies inherited them from Greco-Roman Antiquity where they were used to justify colonization and subjugation (Isaac, *The Invention of Racism in Classical Antiquity*). This was one of the ways in which the human mind dealt with the exploitation of its own kind, by considering them as distinct, "foreigners," and inferior, in short not like one's own kind. But in spite of their distinctiveness and inferiority, their economic importance made the enslaved part of medieval societies and turned integration and manumission into a necessity. Since economic exploitation went hand in hand with sociocultural inclusion of the enslaved, "origin," "ethnicity," "colour," and "faith" were also regarded as flexible, mutable, and adaptable. The inclusion of enslaved foreigners meant a conversion of their faith and their integration into the new society. Their distinct origin and faith were important because they enabled enslavers to convert the enslaved into their own society. In other words, the act of conversion connected the migration of foreigners to the form of their enslavement, and formed a triangle: migration—enslavement—conversion. This triangle continued to be practised in different forms

---

32 Ibn Buṭlān, "Risāla," 351–52; trans. in A. Mez, *The Renaissance of Islam*, trans. S. K. Bakhsh and D. S. Margoliouth (London: Luzac, 1937), 161–62.

around the Mediterranean and the Near East from Iberia to Iraq throughout the second millennium, and was finally suppressed by the Brussels Conference Act of 1890.[33] Now, more than a century later it is today impossible to denote, as a general rule, which inhabitants of Europe and the Middle East are descendent of slaves.

Conclusion

To draw some conclusions on the connection between migration and slavery, we need to look for the conditions which joined them together to generate a large-scale forced movement of people in the medieval world. Firstly, we have seen how socioeconomic expansion of the private as well as the public spheres depended on enslavement. Secondly, social subjugation went together with the integration of foreigners who had no social ties. And thirdly, the special religious aspect of the medieval world made infidels the most suitable victim. All this generated human trafficking on a transnational scale.

Societies that depend on foreigners for their socioeconomic dynamics will encourage the reception of migrants. Slavery and other extreme forms of social dependency are found particularly in societies where labour is a commodity. However, the medieval transnational network of slaveries was aimed less at the exploitation of the labour of forced migrants than their social integration in versatile ways that benefited the enslaver. Forced migrants were enslaved because of that versatility. Distinct systems of slavery ensured their dependency as forced migrants while transnational trafficking ensured that their integration into the social fabric as freedmen would continue this cycle. The fact that the demand for human merchandise came from the wealthiest medieval societies was used by the people of Eastern Europe, Northern Europe, the Caucasus, Central Europe, and sub-Saharan

---

33 Ehud R. Toledano, *The Ottoman Slave Trade and Its Suppression, 1840–1890* (Princeton: Princeton University Press, 1982).

Africa to profit from the trade in humans, which for them was an abundant commodity.

The economic disparity between wealthy economies which depended on one hand on the integration of migrants as slaves to increase their wealth, and on the other on under-developed economies for whom human trafficking was the main means to acquire wealth, brought about this exchange. Human trafficking was a way to distribute wealth between less developed and more developed economies. Yet, enslaving and commodifying human beings connected economies and people in a violent way. Thus, enslavement, trafficking, and migration, created social, economic, and cultural links between distinct medieval worlds, and expanded geopolitically the medieval economic map.

An increasing interest in the situation of forced migrants today leads us to acknowledge the international economic framework of transnational movements of people. Our analysis of the medieval system of enslavement and migration shows us that human trafficking and transnational enslavement are possible because they link distinct socioeconomic systems under a shared global logic.

Conclusion

Slavery as Historical Process—
Towards a New Definition

The previous chapters have examined different phenomena of persons, societies, and cultures enslaving others and
they have revealed the ways that they were systematized.
The long-term historical perspective adopted in this study
has revealed the ways in which slavery was connected to
the development of distinct societies during the period of
their formation and transformation. Enslavement of human
beings was not just a part of the major historical processes
of Mediterranean, European, and Middle Eastern societies in
the first millennium, but played a constitutive role in their
development. One of the main conclusions to draw from this
study is that slavery operates as a system: it provides legal
structures for acts of enslavement, adapts itself to the socioeconomic setting, and also justifies itself within a cultural and
ideological context.

We normally refer to slavery in the singular. However, the
complexity and diversity of societies, economies, polities,
and cultures of the first millennium resulted in very diverse
forms of slavery. This diversity was a product of different
conditions, circumstances, and needs that created different
forms of enslavement for different purposes; this shows the
adaptable and versatile character of the system of slavery.
We therefore need to refer to slaveries in the plural, and to
understand the ways they are connected to processes of
change and transformation, that is, to understand slavery as
a historical process. By adapting the forms of socioeconomic

subjugation to changing circumstances, systems of slavery develop, change, and grow. The fact that this is done by exploiting and abusing human beings, and by using extreme violence and domination over them, does not prevent slavery from becoming central to processes of development. On the contrary, the legitimation of the use of severe force, violence, and coercion is what allows slavery to flourish.

Enslavement is an act of violence. It changes forever the status and state of a human being, whether born or made enslaved. Persons who sell or bind themselves, or participate in their enslavement as active agents, no matter what the reasons and motivations may be, are not enslaving themselves, but are being enslaved by others. Slavery is the system that allows acts of enslavement to happen, legitimizing, institutionalizing, and sustaining them. The societies we have been studying used such systems as means for their development. Slavery is not the result of social, economic, and political processes. It generates them.

Can this historical perspective help us understand phenomena of enslavement that are termed today "modern slavery"? Is slavery really back, and if yes what kind of slavery and how can we fight it? For these questions the historical study that reveals slavery as multifaceted system, a versatile form of violence, adaptable to changing circumstances and needs, is indeed helpful. It shows us the conditions on which systems of slavery depend and the objectives that they serve. We can thus distinguish between different forms of enslavement and identify the circumstances and reasons that make them into a system. In the societies of the first millennium systems of slavery functioned in vacuums, or in zones of difference: between the private and the public, between different types of legal systems, between enslavement *de facto* and *de jure*, between advanced and less-advanced economies. Slavery needs such vacuums because it acts on, and is fed by, economic inequality. Slavery makes this inequality formative to processes of development. For this matter it is not crucial whether slavery constitutes thirty percent or ten percent of the economic activities in a given society. This is also the reason why this study has avoided attempts to estimate the number of slaves. Once a system of slavery makes enslavement formative to processes of development, it becomes useful and sometimes even essential as a method of change. The question about modern slavery, therefore, can and should be differently posed: can we identify today new systems that enable and encourage acts of enslavement which serve socioeconomic processes? The answer is yes.

The previous chapters show slavery as instrumental for the formation and development of very different societies throughout history. Moreover, movements of people, coercion, and commodification of an individual's life, labour, and status, became a means of connectivity between different societies in a global economic framework. We can observe how in today's world two distinct phenomena combine to create conditions that encourage enslavement. On one hand the distribution of wealth has made work and living conditions unviable. The exploitation of people, their life, and work has become a major resource for economic development. On the other hand, when combined with an unstable political situation, people can be displaced in large numbers and we see mass migration of workers (national or cross-national), refugees, human trafficking and smuggling which in turn encourages the dispensability of workers, and the very value of their life and work. All these can count as forced migration.

Why do these two phenomena that feed one another generate conditions that encourage enslavement? The movement of workers and the precariousness of their work create a situation in which they are both included and excluded. Their destination societies incorporate them as workers while maintaining a distinct status for them as foreigners. Such workers are social outsiders through a separate and unfavourable civic status. The result is a hierarchy within the labour market, defined by the law. The labour market and its evolution become conditioned and determined by the legal status of the worker. This does not apply to foreigners alone. Other precarious states of human existence, such as extreme poverty, dispensability of human beings, and the value of their work and life, create, even encourage, conditions to employ enslavement as a means of economic growth.

When socioeconomic units become dependent on forms of enslavement for their development, we can argue that a system of slavery has been formed. Slavery as a system creates the conditions for personal forms of dependency in the private sphere and for using them for economic development. In this way acts of enslavement become vital and difficult to fight and eradicate, in contrast to sporadic private acts of enslavement that are easily banned and eliminated. The following five criteria help us to discern when acts of enslavement become systematized. All five were decisive criteria in systems of slavery in the societies of the first millennium:

- *Enslavement as a means of generating socioeconomic dynamism*
  Acts of enslavement become fundamental to the economy when they are used to create social structures of inequality and dependency. They help economic development because they normalize exploitation as part of the social structure. This generates socioeconomic dynamics based on inequality and dependency in various economic settings, family-based, plantation-like, industrial or small-scale.

- *Legal definitions that establish a separate civil status for the enslaved*
  The enslaved persons are defined by a particular status that sets a legal distinction between them and other members of society. It need not be a designated legal definition. Bondage, for example, is a legal condition that sets a distinct legal status by restricting the rights of the bound person in relation to other members of society.

- *The coexistence of forms of inclusion and exclusion of the enslaved*
  Forms of inclusion of enslaved persons into society determine how they are defined as members of society (inclusion) and also as outsiders (exclusion). They provide ways

to integrate the enslaved, determine the level of their dependency, subjugation, and exploitation, and how and when the enslaved will be excluded from certain social relations and dynamics.

- *Personal conditions particular to the enslaved*
  The civil status of the enslaved determines their personal conditions and restrict what we perceive today as freedom (though freedom as a civil and political concept is a construct of the last three centuries). Freedom had no legal definition in the first millennium other than not being a slave. It is impossible to evaluate enslavement by its "distance from freedom" or as "unfreedom," an undefined concept used by historians to cover an amalgam of statuses which do not conform to the modern definition of freedom. Rather, we need to focus on the particular personal conditions that distinguish the enslaved from other members of society, including their ability and inability to change their status and exercise agency.

- *Cultural and ideological justification of enslavement*
  Ideologies and mindsets define the way acts of enslavement, their violence, and forms of control are perceived. They determine public opinion and the place of human rights. Slavery as a system cannot exist without moral and psychological justifications. We need to identify the cultural and ideological elements that create the mindsets that support and justify enslavement as well as the exclusion of the enslaved from society. They provide meaning to acts of enslavement, personal conditions, and the special civil status of the enslaved. They play a central role in making slavery a system.

If I were to propose a new definition of slavery based on these five criteria and the role it played in the formation of medieval societies, it would be the following one: slavery is a social system that encourages, supports, and institutionalizes acts of enslavement (the ownership, possession, commodification of human beings or their work). Second, the institutionalization of acts of enslavement transforms the power relations in society by creating forms of private subjects. It enables a change in relations between public and private power, and this makes up the system that supports it as historical process.

If we return to the images of slavery that we evoked right at the beginning of this book, we have acquired a methodology to understand them in a much broader context and to acknowledge the different aspects in which slavery was beneficial to the development of their respective societies. We have shown how slavery functions as a system. We perceive and define slavery today as a crime against humanity and fight for its eradication. This cannot be done without understanding slavery's role and function as a socioeconomic engine of development and as a historical process. If we wish to eradicate it, we need to change or replace the ways in which acts of enslavement are systematized through the five criteria just listed, and propose and promote alternative means of social and economic development.

Further Reading

Primary Sources

Greek and Latin

Actes d'Iviron. Edited by Jacques Lefort, Denise Papachryss-anthou, and Nicolas Oikonomidès. 4 vols. Paris: Lethielleux, 1985–1995.

Codex Theodosianus. Edited by Theodor Mommsen. 2 vols. in 3. Repr. of 2nd ed. 1954 (orig. 1905). Berlin: Weidmann, 1962.

Corpus iuris ciuilis. Vol. 1, *Codex Justinianus*. Edited by Paul Krüger. Hildesheim: Weidmann, 1877. (Online translation at https://droitromain.univ-grenoble-alpes.fr/Anglica/codjust_Scott.htm.)

——— . Vol. 1, *Institutiones [Justiniani]*. Edited by Paul Krüger and Theodor Mommsen. 16th ed. Hildesheim: Weidmann, 1954.

——— . *The Digest of Justinian*. Trans. Alan Watson (of *Digesta Justiniani*, ed. by Paul Krüger and Theodor Mommsen). 4 vols. Philadelphia: University of Pennsylvania Press, 1985.

——— . Vol. 3, *Novellae [Justiniani]*. Edited by R. Schoell. 8th ed. Repr., 1993; Hildesheim: Weidmann, 1963.

The Latin *Corpus Iuris Civilis* was issued in three parts on the request of Emperor Justinian in 529–534. The *Codex Justinianus* compiled all of the extant imperial *constitutiones* from the time of Hadrian. The second part, the *Digest* (*Digesta*) issued in 533, compiled writings of the great Roman jurists and current edicts. The third part, the *Institutes* (*Institutiones*), was a sort of legal textbook. Later, Justinian issued other laws, mostly in Greek, which were called *Novels* (*Novellae*).

Gregory the Great. *Registrum epistularum*. Edited by D. L. Norberg. 2 vols. (*Libri I–VII* and *Libri VIII–XIV*.) Corpus Christianorum Series Latina 140 and 140A. Turnhout: Brepols, 1982.

The Institutes of Gaius. Translated by W. M. Gordon and O. F. Robinson (with the Latin edition of E. Seckel and B. Kuebler). London: Duckworth, 1988.

The Institutes of Justinian see Corpus iuris civilis.

Jerome. "The Life of Malchus the Captive." In Jerome, *Trois Vies de moines (Paul, Malchus, Hilarion)*. Edited by Edgardo Martín Morales. Translated by Pierre Leclerc. Paris: Cerf, 2007.

Josephus, Flavius. "De bello Iudaico." In vol. 6 of *Flavii Iosephi opera*. Edited by B. Niese. Repr. 1995; Berlin: Weidmann, 1895.

Jus Graecoromanum. Edited by I. Zepos and P. Zepos. 8 vols. Athens: Fexīs, 1931; repr. Darmstadt: Scientia, 1962.

Maspero, Jean. *Papyrus grecs d'époque byzantine, Catalogue général des antiquités égyptiennes du Musée du Caire*, 3 vols. Cairo: Institut français d'Archéologie orientale, 1910–1916.

Novellae Justiniani see Corpus iuris civilis.

Noy, David. *Jewish Inscriptions of Western Europe*. 2 vols. (Cambridge: Cambridge University Press, 1993).

Petronius Arbiter. *Satyricon*. Translated by Michael Heseltine and revised by E. H. Warmington. Loeb Classical Library 15. Cambridge, MA: Harvard University Press, 1913.

Procopius. *De bello Gothico*. Vol. 3, *Historia quae dicitur arcana* of *Procopii Caesariensis opera omnia*. Edited by J. Haury. Leipzig: Teubner, 1963. English translation by H. B. Dewing available online at Project Gutenberg.

——. *De bello Persico*. Vols. 1–2, *De bellis libri I–IV* and *De bellis libri V–VIII* of *Procopii Caesariensis opera omnia*. Edited by J. Haury. Leipzig: Teubner, 1962–1963. English translation by H. B. Dewing available online at Project Gutenberg.

Arabic

al-Balādhurī. *Kitāb Futūh al-Buldān*. Edited by U. A. al-Tabbā and 'A. A. Ṭabbā'. Beirut: Dār al-Nashr li-al-Jāmi'īyīn, 1957. (Trans. Philip Hitti, *The Book of the Conquest of Lands*. New York: Columbia University Press, 1916.)

Ibn Buṭlān. "Risālā fī shirā' al-raqīq wa-taqlīb al-'abīd." In *Nawādir al-makhṭūṭāṭ*, edited by 'Abd Salām Hārūn, 4: 351–89. 4 vols. Cairo: Musṭafā al-Bābī al-Ḥalabī, 1954.

Ibn Faḍlān, Aḥmad. *Mission to the Volga*. Translated by James E. Montgomery. Edited by Shawkat M. Toorawa. New York: NYU Press, 2017.

Ibn Ḥawkal. *La configuration de la Terre / Kitab surat al-ard*. Edited by J. H. Kramers and G. Wiet. 2 vols. Paris: Maisonneuve et Larose, 2001.

Ibn 'Idhārī. *Kitāb al-bayān al-mughrib fī akhbār al-Andalus was al-Maghrib*. Edited by G. S. Colin and E. Lévi-Provençal. 2 vols. Paris: Geuthner, 1930.

Rāġib, Yūsuf. *Actes de vente d'esclaves et d'animaux d'Egypte médiévale*. 2 vols. Cairo: Institut français d'archéologie orientale, 2002–2006.

Serjeant, R. B. "The Sunnah Jāmi'ah, Pacts with the Yathrib: Analysis and Translation of the Documents Comprised in the So-called 'Constitution of Medina'." *Bulletin of the School of Oriental and African Studies* 41 (1978): 1–42.

al-Ṭabarī. *The History of al-Ṭabarī / Ta'rīkh al-rusul wa'l-mulūk*.

——. Vol. 35, *The Crisis of the 'Abbāsid Caliphate: The Caliphates of al-Mustaʿīn and al-Muʿtazz, A.D. 862–869/A.H. 248–255*. Translated by George Saliba. SUNY Series in Near Eastern Studies. Albany, NY: State University of New York Press, 1985.

——. Vol. 36, *The Revolt of the Zanj A.D. 869–879/A.H. 255–265*. Translated by David Waines. SUNY Series in Near Eastern Studies. Albany, NY: State University of New York Press, 1992.

Hebrew, Aramaic, and Judeo-Arabic

Babylonian Talmud *see* "Responsa" Project.

Goitein, S. D. *Letters of Medieval Jewish Traders*. Princeton: Princeton University Press, 1973.

Mann, Jacob. *Texts and Studies in Jewish History and Literature*. 2 vols. Cincinnati: Hebrew Union College Press, 1931–1935.

Mishnah *see* "Responsa" Project.

"Responsa" Project, Bar Ilan University: www.biu.ac.il/en/about-bar-ilan/jewish-heritage/responsa-project.

A global database of 100,000 Torah rulings including a large Responsa collection of questions and answers, the Bible, the Babylonian Talmud and Jerusalem Talmud and their commentaries, the Midrash, the Zohar, Halachic Law (Rambam, Tur, Shulchan Aruch), the Talmudic Encyclopedia, and other sources.

Tosefta *see* "Responsa" Project.

Secondary Literature

Antiquity

Andreau, Jean and Raymond Descat. *The Slave in Greece and Rome*. Translated by Marion Leopolod. Madison: University of Wisconsin Press, 2011.

Bradley, Keith. "On Captives under the Principate." *Phoenix* 58, no. 3–4 (2004): 298–318.

Buckland, W. W. *The Roman Law of Slavery*. Cambridge: Cambridge University Press, 1970.

De Wet, Chris L. *The Unbound God: Slavery and the Formation of Early Christian Thought*. London: Routledge, 2018.

Fitzgerald, W. *Slavery and the Roman Literary Imagination*. Cambridge: Cambridge University Press, 2000.

Garnsey, Peter. *Ideas of Slavery from Aristotle to Augustine*. Cambridge: Cambridge University Press, 1996.

Glancy, Jennifer. *Slavery in Early Christianity*. Oxford: Oxford University Press, 2002.

Harper, Kyle. *Slavery in the Late Roman World, AD 275–425*. Cambridge: Cambridge University Press, 2011.

Isaac, Benjamin. *The Invention of Racism in Classical Antiquity*. Princeton: Princeton University Press, 2004.

Klingshirn, William. "Caesarius of Arles and the Ransoming of Captives in Sub-Roman Gaul." *Journal of Roman Studies* 75 (1985): 183–203.

Scheidel, Walter. "The Roman Slave Supply." In *The Cambridge World History of Slavery*, vol. 1, *The Ancient Mediterranean World*, edited by Keith Bradley and Paul Cartledge, 287–310. Cambridge: Cambridge University Press, 2011.

Middle Ages

Ayalon, David. *Islam and the Abode of War: Military Slaves and Islamic Adversaries*. Variorum Collected Studies 456. Aldershot: Ashgate, 1994.

Bacharach, Jere L. "African Military Slaves in the Medieval Middle East: The Cases of Iraq (869–955) and Egypt (868–1171)." *International Journal of Middle East Studies* 13 (1981): 471–95.

Berger, Lutz. "Mamluks in Abbasid Society." In *Migration History of the Medieval Afro-Eurasian Transition Zone*, edited by L. Renfandt, J. Preiser-Kapeller, and I. Stouraitis, 413–29. Leiden: Brill, 2020.

Bloch, Marc. "Comment et pourquoi finit l'esclavage antique." *Annales ESC* 2, no. 2 (1947): 161–70.

Crone, Patricia. *Slaves on Horses: The Evolution of the Islamic Polity*. Cambridge: Cambridge University Press, 1980.

Epstein, Steven A. *Speaking of Slavery: Color, Ethnicity, and Human Bondage in Italy*. Ithaca: Cornell University Press, 2001.

Franz, Kurt. "Slavery in Islam: Legal Norms and Social Practice." In *Slavery and the Slave Trade in the Eastern Mediterranean (ca. 1000–1500 CE)*, edited by Reuven Amitai and Christoph Cluse, 51–142. Turnhout: Brepols, 2017.

Goitein, Shlomo Dov. *A Mediterranean Society: The Jewish Communities of the Arab World as Portrayed in the Documents of the Cairo Geniza*. 6 vols. Berkeley: University of California Press, 1967–1993.

Gordon, Matthew S. *The Breaking of a Thousand Swords: A History of the Turkish Military of Samarra (AH 200–275/815–889 CE)*. Albany: State University of New York Press, 2001.

——. "Unhappy Offspring? Concubines and Their Sons in Early Abbasid Society." *International Journal of Middle East Studies* 49, no. 1 (2017): 153–57.

Gordon, Murray. *Slavery in the Arab World*. New York: New Amsterdam, 1989.

Karras, Ruth Mazo. *Slavery and Society in Medieval Scandinavia*. New Haven: Yale University Press, 1988.

Lemerle, Paul. *Cinq études sur le XIᵉ s. byzantin*. Paris: CNRS, 1977.

McCormick, Michael. *Origins of the European Economy: Communications and Commerce, AD 300–900*. Cambridge: Cambridge University Press, 2001.

Meouak, Mohamed. *Ṣaqâliba: eunuques et esclaves à la conquête du pouvoir. géographie et histoire des élites politiques "marginales" dans l'Espagne umayyade*. Helsinki: Academia scientiarum Fennica, 2004.

Pelteret, David. *Slavery in Early Mediaeval England*. Woodbridge: Boydell, 1995.

Pipes, Daniel. *Slave Soldiers and Islam: The Genesis of a Military System*. New Haven: Yale University Press, 1981.

Rio, Alice. *Slavery after Rome, 500–1100*. Oxford: Oxford University Press, 2017.

Rotman, Youval. *Byzantine Slavery and the Mediterranean World*. Translated by J. M. Todd. Cambridge, MA: Harvard University Press, 2009.

—— . "Captives and Redeeming Captives: The Law and the Community." In *Judaea/Palaestina, Babylon and Rome: Jews in the Roman, Parthian and Sassanian Empire*, edited by Benjamin Isaac, Y. Shahar, 227–48. Tübingen: Mohr Siebeck, 2012.

—— . "The Map of the Medieval Slave Trade." *H-Slavery Resources*, edited by D. Prior (available since 2018 at https://networks.h-net.org/system/files/contributed-files/yrotman2cmedievalhumantrafficking2cmapanddata.pdf).

Savage, E. "Berbers and Blacks: Ibadi Slave Traffic in Eighth-Century North Africa." *Journal of African History* 33, no. 3 (1992): 351–68.

Trabelsi, Salah. "Commerce et esclavage dans le Maghreb oriental (VIIe–Xe siècles)." In *Couleurs de l'esclavage sur les deux rives de la Méditerranée (Moyen Age–XXe siècle)*, edited by Roger Botte and Alessandro Stella, 9–23. Paris: Karthala, 2012.

Wickham, Chris. *Framing the Early Middle Ages: Europe and the Mediterranean 400–800*. Oxford: Oxford University Press, 2005.

Modern and the Contemporary World

Allain, Jean, ed. *The Legal Understanding of Slavery: From the Historical to the Contemporary*. Oxford: Oxford University Press, 2012.

Bales, Kevin. *Disposable People: New Slavery in the Global Economy*. Los Angeles: University of California Press, 1999.

Bogner, Artur and Gabriele Rosenthal. *Child Soldiers in Context: Biographies, Familial and Collective Trajectories in Northern Uganda*. Göttingen: Göttingen University Press, 2020. https://doi.org/10.17875/gup2020–1325.

Bravo, Karen E. "Exploring the Analogy between Modern Trafficking in Humans and the Trans-Atlantic Slave Trade." *Boston University International Law Journal* 25, no. 2 (2007), 207–96. https://www.bu.edu/law/journals-archive/international/volume25n2/documents/207-296.pdf

Eltis, David. *The Rise of African Slavery in the Americas*. Cambridge: Cambridge University Press, 2000.

Miller, Joseph. *The Problem of Slavery as History: A Global Approach*. New Haven: Yale University Press, 2018.

Kotiswaran, Prabha, ed. *Revisiting the Law and Governance of Trafficking, Forced Labor and Modern Slavery*. Cambridge: Cambridge University Press, 2017.

Shelley, Louise. *Human Trafficking: A Global Perspective*. Cambridge: Cambridge University Press, 2010.

Zeuske, Michael. *Sklaverei: Eine Menschheitsgeschichte von der Steinzeit bis heute*. Ditzingen: Reclam, 2018.

Anthropology and Sociology

Castles, Stephen. "Towards a Sociology of Forced Migration and Social Transformation", *Sociology* 37, no. 1 (2003): 13-34.

Condominas, Georges L., ed. *Formes extrêmes de dépendance: Contributions à l'étude de l'esclavage en Asie du Sud-Est*. Paris: EHESS, 1988.

Meillasoux, Claude. *The Anthropology of Slavery: The Womb of Iron and Gold*. Translated by A. Dasnois. Chicago: The University of Chicago Press, 1991.

Miers, Suzanne. "Slavery: A Question of Definition." *Slavery and Abolition* 24, no. 2 (2003): 1–6.

Miers, Suzanne and Igor Kopytoff, eds. *Slavery in Africa: Historical and Anthropological Perspectives*. Madison: University of Wisconsin Press, 1977.

Quirk, Joel and Darshan Vigneswaran, eds. *Slavery, Migration and Contemporary Bondage in Africa*. Trenton: Africa World, 2013.

Reports and Conventions

The Bellagio–Harvard Guidelines on the Legal Parameters of Slavery (2012). Available online at various locations including https://glc.yale.edu/sites/default/files/pdf/the_bellagio-_harvard_guidelines_on_the_legal_parameters_of_slavery.pdf.

General Assembly of the United Nations, "The Protocol to Prevent, Suppress and Punish Trafficking in Persons Especially Women and Children, supplementing the United Nations Convention against Transnational Organized Crime," resolution 55/25 of 15 November 2000: https://www.ohchr.org/en/professionalinterest/pages/protocoltraffickinginpersons.aspx.

International Labour Organization and Walk Free Foundation, "Global Estimates of Modern Slavery" (2017): http://www.ilo.org/wcmsp5/groups/public/@dgreports/@dcomm/documents/publication/wcms_575479.pdf.

League of Nations, "The Convention to Suppress the Slave Trade and Slavery" (1926): https://www.ohchr.org/Documents/ProfessionalInterest/slavery.pdf.

U.S. Department of State, "2018 Trafficking in Persons Report" (July 2018): https://www.state.gov/j/tip/rls/tiprpt/2018/.

UK Home Office, "Modern Slavery: statutory guidance for England and Wales (under s49 of the Modern Slavery Act 2015) and non-statutory guidance for Scotland and Northern Ireland":   https://assets.publishing.service.gov.uk/government/uploads/system/uploads/attachment_data/file/509326/victims-of-modern-slavery-frontline-staff-guidance-v3.pdf.

Modern Court Cases

The Queen v Wei Tang (2006): case at: https://www.hcourt.gov.au/assets/publications/judgment-summaries/2008/hca39-2008-08-28.pdf (accessed April 1, 2020). The law is at   https://www.legislation.gov.au/Details/C2004A00495 (accessed November 1, 2020).

United States of America v Mohamed Toure, Denise Cros-Toure (2020):   https://www.justice.gov/crt/case-document/file/1242061/download (accessed March 3, 2020). https://www.justice.gov/opa/pr/texas-couple-each-sentenced-seven-years-prison-forced-labor-and-related-offenses (accessed April 1, 2020).